D0949817

TODAY'S TOP
LEADERS HAIL
LINCOLN ON LEADERSHIP

more...

★

"Sound advice...[a] superb book."

—Norman R. Augustine,
  CEO, Martin Marietta Corporation

★

"A nugget of wisdom can be found on every page....I'm still taking notes!"

—Reuben Mark,
  Chairman, Colgate-Palmolive

★

"This is an absolutely fascinating, instructive and inspiring look into the heart, mind and style of a truly principle-centered leader."

—Stephen R. Covey,
  author of *The Seven Habits of Highly Effective People*

★

"Lucid...compelling...a book not to be missed by anyone who manages people and problems."

—James M. McPherson,
  author of *Battle Cry of Freedom* and
  Abraham Lincoln and the Second American Revolution

★

"I highly recommend it....Many of the lessons it took me years to learn are contained in *Lincoln on Leadership*."

—Joe Paterno,
  Head Football Coach, Penn State University

★

"*Lincoln on Leadership* not only addresses sound management principles, but personifies them in a way that makes their application clear and straightforward."

—Frank Popoff,
  President and CEO, Dow Chemical Company

★

"Phillips shows vividly that Lincoln certainly understood...
the basic precepts of leadership."

—Lt. Gen. (Ret.) Dave R. Palmer,
  Superintendent, United States Military Academy, 1986–1991

★

"Phillips has provided a fascinating and shrewd portrait of
Lincoln as a leader."

—James O. Freedman,
  President, Dartmouth College

★

"For anyone whose job is motivating and inspiring others,
this book is indispensable."

—Lou Holtz,
  Head Football Coach, University of Notre Dame

★

"I heartily recommend it. It's an excellent primer for
corporate executives who are striving to lead a major
culture change within their own organizations."

—Raymond W. Smith,
  Chairman and CEO, Bell Atlantic Corporation

★

"Mr. Phillips exhibits extraordinary talent and scholarship...
[a] magnificent manual of wise leadership."

—United States Senator **Don Nickles**

★

"This book's gripping and brilliant description of Lincoln's
approach to leadership and its relevance to modern
management concerns should be required reading for
anyone who wants to lead."

—Burt Nanus,
  author of *The Leader's Edge* and co-author of
  Leaders: The Strategies of Taking Charge

★   *more...*

"Fascinating reading…it conveys a very significant message to those of us who have that concern of being leaders for others."
—William K. Coors,
President, Adolph Coors Company

"Well-organized…easy to follow.…So many of Lincoln's principles apply to athletics in general.…Once I started *Lincoln on Leadership,* I was hooked."
—Larry Smith,
Head Football Coach, University of Southern California

"Invaluable lessons that deserve careful study by all those who bear the responsibility to lead contemporary society."
—United States Senator **David L. Boren**

"Very informative…made me think about Lincoln's leadership style and his strategies that apply to our situation today."
—Tom Osborne,
Head Football Coach, University of Nebraska

"A very, very good read. Lincoln's leadership style is a model for how business leaders should behave."
—P. W. J. Wood,
President, Energy Exploration Management Company

★

Phillips makes astute observations on Lincoln's style of leadership.…Managers who need to be leaders in times of crisis would do well to study Lincoln."
—Jeff Cox,
author of *The Goal, Zapp!,* and *The Quadrant Solution*

LINCOLN ON LEADERSHIP

EXECUTIVE STRATEGIES
· FOR TOUGH TIMES ·

DONALD T. PHILLIPS

WARNER BOOKS

A Time Warner Company

Warner Books, Inc., 1271 Avenue of the Americas, New York, NY 10020

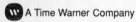 A Time Warner Company

Printed in the United States of America
First trade printing: February 1993
        15 16 17 18 19 20

Library of Congress Cataloging-in-Publication Data

Phillips, Don T.
    Lincoln on leadership : executive strategies for tough times / by
Donald T. Phillips.
        p.   cm.
    Includes bibliographical references and index.
    ISBN 0-446-39459-9
    1. Lincoln, Abraham, 1809–1865—Views on political leadership.
2. Political leadership—United States.   I. Title.
E457.2.P54   1992
973.7'092—dc20
                                                                91-50076
                                                                CIP

Book design by Giorgetta Bell McRee
Cover design by Mario Pulice
Cover illustration by Mark Weakly

Excerpts from *Leadership* by James MacGregor Burns. Copyright © 1978 by James MacGregor Burns. Reprinted by permission of HarperCollins Publishers. / Excerpts from *The Collected Works of Abraham Lincoln*, edited by Roy P. Basler. Copyright © 1953 by the Abraham Lincoln Association. Reprinted with permission of Rutgers University Press. / Excerpts from *Leaders: The Strategies for Taking Charge* by Warren Bennis and Burt Nanus, Copyright © 1982 by Warren Bennis and Burt Nanus. Reprinted by permission of HarperCollins Publishers. / Excerpts from *On Leadership* by John W. Gardner, Copyright © 1990 by John W. Gardner. Reprinted by permission of The Free Press, a Division of Macmillan, Inc. / Excerpts from *Lincoln's Wartime Leadership: The First Hundred Days; Journal of the Abraham Lincoln Association*, by Don E. Fehrenbacher, vol. 9, 1987. Copyright © 1987 by Board of Trustees, University of Illinois. Reprinted by permission of University of Illinois Press. / Excerpts from *In Search of Excellence* by Thomas J. Peters and Robert H. Waterman, Jr. Copyright © 1982 by Thomas J. Peters and Robert H. Waterman, Jr. Reprinted by permission of HarperCollins Publishers. / Excerpts reprinted by permission of Louisiana State University Press from *Abraham Lincoln: Public Speaker* by Waldo W. Braden. Copyright © 1988 by Louisiana State University Press. / Excerpts from *With Malice Toward None* by Stephen B. Oates. Copyright © 1977 by Stephen B. Oates. Reprinted by permission of HarperCollins Publishers. / Excerpts from *The Abraham Lincoln Encyclopedia* by Mark E. Neely, Jr. Copyright © 1982 by McGraw-Hill, Inc. Reproduced with permission of McGraw-Hill, Inc. / Excerpts from *Abe Lincoln Laughing* by P.M. Zall. Copyright © 1982 by Univ. of California Press, Berkeley. Reprinted by permission of the author.

For my sons,
Steven and David

Contents

Preface

One day in 1983, as I was leaving town to attend a week-long management seminar, I happened to grab a volume of Carl Sandburg's *Lincoln: The War Years* to help fill the sometimes long, idle hours that such retreats can spawn. About halfway through the seminar I began to notice that Abraham Lincoln, as president of the United States, seemed to use many of the methods that were being recommended to us in the class. My curiosity piqued, I devoured the remainder of the book I'd brought along, discovering that indeed Lincoln seemed to be a model for much of what was being taught. In class we were being told such things as: "Get out of the Ivory Tower and get to know your people. It's the only way you can know what is really happening in your department." In my hotel room Sandburg was telling me that Lincoln visited Generals Burnside at Fredericksburg, McClellan at Antietam, and Hooker at Chancellorsville in order to get a better handle on the war effort.

Later, to improve my own managerial skills, I decided to explore this aspect of Abraham Lincoln's life in more detail. I assumed there would be numerous books and articles on his leadership and management style. I was surprised, though, to find that the local library had nothing on the subject. When I contacted the Abraham Lincoln Bookshop in Chicago and said that I was looking for a book on a very specific aspect of Lincoln's life, the proprietor informed me that he could supply me with a book on every conceivable subject dealing with our sixteenth president. "What specific subject are you looking for?" asked Dan Weinberg. "Leadership or management philosophy," I replied. "Sorry," said Dan, "no one has yet written a book on that particular aspect of Lincoln."

I subsequently contacted the Lewis A. Warren Lincoln Library in Fort Wayne, Indiana, and requested copies of any articles or papers that dealt with Lincoln and leadership. They sent me three: one written in 1895 by Noah Brooks (a contemporary of Lincoln's), another that was an excerpt from a speech given to the Lincoln Society of Taiwan, and another that had to do primarily with an unrelated discussion of Lee and Grant. It was now quite obvious to me that if I were to learn anything about this particular subject. I would have to research it on my own.

And that is how this book began. Before I knew it, I'd accumulated a mountain of information. In organizing it, I began to notice striking patterns in Lincoln's style. For example, I observed that Lincoln's anecdotes could very easily be cataloged under various headings that reveal much of the man's personality and exceptional understanding of people, not to mention his leadership philosophy. Moreover, years of researching Lincoln's speeches and writings revealed these same recurring patterns in even greater detail.

To properly write this book I had to become more than just a Lincoln buff; I had to become a student of Lincoln. Further,

I had to become a student of leadership as well. In my own corporate environment, employing what I'd learned yielded amazingly positive results. My department was more productive, more successful, and my staff enjoyed their work with a passion. Overall, it was the examination of Lincoln's performance as a leader, through tangible, visceral examples, that helped me better understand the complicated theories of leadership.

Having been in the business world for many years now, mostly in large corporate settings, I am still confounded and amazed that, of the hundreds of managers and supervisors I've encountered, I can count on one hand the number of real leaders among them. Many of these men and women are corrupted by power; most tend to pressure or dictate when simple suggestions or recommendations would suffice. And almost always there is a lack of understanding of the simple points of human nature, such as a person's reaction at being ordered to do something rather than being asked his or her opinion.

Perhaps true leadership is uncommon in today's society because it's not genuinely understood and has often been misinterpreted. James McGregor Burns, author of the book *Leadership*, followed this line of thinking when he wrote:

> Many acts heralded or bemoaned as instances of leadership—acts of oratory, manipulation, sheer self-advancement, brute coercion—are not such. Much of what commonly passes as leadership—conspicuous position-taking without followers or follow-through, posturing on various public stages, manipulation without general purpose, authoritarianism—is no more leadership than the behavior of small boys marching in front of a parade, who continue to strut along Main Street after the procession has turned down a side street toward the fairgrounds.

Why are there so few leaders in today's business community? The answer seems to be that most managers simply don't understand or know enough about the nuts and bolts of skilled leadership. It's a difficult subject to master because there are no specifics that can be taught. And it is even more arduous to implement because doing so often involves trial and failure, pain and discomfort.

Since leadership principles are usually expressed rather abstractly, there is a great need for simple, concrete illustrations. Tangible examples make the difference; people relate to them. That's what the study of Lincoln gives us—tangible examples from a widely recognized great leader. Therein lies the basic premise of this book. I hope that present and future leaders in all walks of life will be enlightened (as I was) by the remarkable leadership genius of Abraham Lincoln and then will use that knowledge to improve their own skills.

While in some instances I've elected to place his statements in today's vernacular, the reader will find much of this book to be in Lincoln's own words. It's subdivided into several key "lessons," each representing an important avenue toward the understanding of Lincoln's personal leadership style.

For most of Lincoln's quotations, I have relied heavily on Roy P. Basler's magnificently well-documented *Collected Works of Abraham Lincoln*. When using this and other sources, I have included only those quotes that I believe reflect Lincoln's leadership philosophy and have left out all that I know to be spurious.

Those quotations written in Lincoln's own hand are easily verified and given great credibility. But what of other quotations that are not as easily documented? Those, for instance, supplied by an individual's memory of conversations with Lincoln. Passed down over the years, this type of quotation may often be a muddled or reworded statement of what Lincoln actually said. The reader should keep this in mind when perusing any story or anecdote attributed to Lincoln.

The reader will note, by the way, that certain Lincoln "principles," cited at the end of each chapter, will not have been introduced previously in the chapter narrative. In all cases, these new principles derive from actual Lincoln quotes relevant to the chapter's theme.

I would like to thank Daniel R. Weinberg and Joseph E. Suppiger for their early encouragement to write and publish on this subject. The staff at the Lewis A. Warren Lincoln Library in Fort Wayne, Indiana, headed by Mark E. Neely, Jr., painstakingly aided me in identifying and verifying many of the quotes used herein. Many members of the Abraham Lincoln Association have also been very supportive. Anthony Del Prete spent numerous hours editing and significantly improving the first draft. The following people read various portions of the manuscript and made many useful suggestions: Mike Lombardo, director of the Center for Creative Leadership in Greensboro, North Carolina, Greg Kelleher, Rich Kochick, David Hunt, and Al Lindsay. Don E. Fehrenbacher and Mario Cuomo took time from their busy schedules to read portions of the first draft and offer much-needed encouragement, for which I'm very grateful. I'm also indebted to Bob Lamb, Charlotte and George Friedline, Don and Alice Phillips, and Timothy and Dawn Kostilnik for their encouragement and support through the years.

Rick Horgan, my editor at Warner Books, made great contributions to the organization of the book and provided his masterful expertise in detailed editing.

Special thinks must also go to Paul R. White, with whom I spent countless hours in conversations that significantly enhanced and enlightened my knowledge and understanding of the art of leadership; and to Dale Hershey, my fellow Lincoln enthusiast, whose scholarly and intuitive understanding of Abraham Lincoln was shared generously throughout this project. Their comments and suggestions pervade the entire work, and words alone cannot express to them how grateful I am for their help.

And, finally, all my love and gratitude to my wife, Susan, and sons, Steven and David, who for many years gave me the encouragement, understanding, and precious time needed to research and write this book.

Introduction

Throughout the relatively brief history of the United States there have been many great leaders. Several, such as Washington, Adams, Jefferson, and the Roosevelts, became presidents; others like Franklin, Webster, Anthony, and King made a dramatic impact on mankind without reaching the White House. There are countless other leaders, on both local and national levels, in all aspects of society, who could be labeled "great." Yet there is one person who rises above all of them. One who is consistently ranked as the greatest president. One who is viewed as the greatest leader this nation has ever known or will ever know. And one who, although dead for more than 125 years, still inspires and moves people from all walks of life, from all around the globe. That person is Abraham Lincoln.

It is not surprising that our vision of Lincoln today is more mythical than real. His role as the embattled Civil War president and "Savior of the Nation" was magnified after his assassination. And with time his enduring image as the Great Emancipator has catapulted him to a level near sainthood. In addition, the labeling of Lincoln as "Honest Abe" and "The Railsplitter" by the media of his time has been perpetuated for well over a century.

Every school-age child in America knows about Abraham Lincoln. Thousands of books and articles have been written on various aspects of his life. Moreover, the image of Lincoln is everywhere. His likeness is on the penny, the five-dollar bill, savings bonds, and certificates of deposit. There are countless statues, photographs, paintings, and sketches of him through-out the United States and around the world. His likeness adorns courtrooms, schools, public buildings, and private residences. There have been plays written about him, along with movies, television programs, magazine articles, songs, and poems. His name has been associated with motels, automobiles, toys, banks, organizations, streets, and objects too numerous to list. In addition, his letters, notes, written speeches, and autographs are in demand all over the world.

With all this exposure ingrained in the American stream of consciousness, it's easy to see why the distance between the myth and the reality of Lincoln is still very wide. In fact, it has only been in the last twenty or thirty years that Lincoln enthusiasts have begun to explore the "real" Lincoln and, at the same time, try to separate and downplay the myth.

Curiously, with everything that has been written about Abraham Lincoln, little is known about his extraordinary leadership ability. This is perhaps because leadership theory itself is a relatively recent phenomenon. Only in the the last ten to fifteen years has the study of leadership been examined closely, and not as part of the "management" philosophy of the business world.

In a way, Abraham Lincoln represented the summation of those leadership qualities that had helped to form a nation. The last great leader before industrial change, Lincoln stood for all that was right, honest, and self-evident. As a boy, his heroes were the Founding Fathers, and he studied the history of that young nation that was so devoted to human rights. He grew up in poverty and had a binding link to the common people. He was innovative at a time when the age of discoveries and inventions was just beginning. He was compassionate and caring yet, when necessary, could put his foot down firmly and be decisive beyond question. He was patient, persistent, consistent, and persuasive rather than dictatorial. But, without a doubt, the foundation of Abraham Lincoln's leadership style was an unshakable commitment to the rights of the individual.

Interestingly, in the many definitions of leadership there are few references to this basic concept of human rights. James MacGregor Burns, in his landmark book *Leadership*, came the closest when he wrote:

> Leadership is leaders inducing followers to act for certain goals that represent *the values* and the motivations—the wants and needs, the aspirations and expectations—of both leaders and followers. And the genius of leadership lies in the manner in which leaders see and act on their own and their *followers' values* and motivations.

As close as Burns comes to a pure definition of leadership, it still seems a shade unfinished or incomplete. Such is the case, however, with virtually every attempt at interpreting, clarifying, or defining the true meaning of leadership. Leadership is an elusive concept that, at times, can be vague and ambiguous. As a result, there are no set rules or formulas for leaders to follow. There are only guidelines and concepts, perceptions and ideas, abstractions and generalities. This is why the art of leading people is so difficult to master and teach, and why there is such a great need for role models. We must study individuals who are recognized as successful leaders, those who have demonstrated their abilities with tangible results. In short, we must look to our heroes. For it is only by examining individuals such as Abraham Lincoln that we can ever hope to understand how effective leadership works.

Studies of other well-known leaders suggest that certain factors in childhood can predispose a person to great leadership. James MacGregor Burns points out, for example, that the most important influences on the shaping of leaders lie "almost wholly in their early years." He observed that Gandhi, Lenin, and Franklin Roosevelt appeared to have "a strong attachment to one parent coupled with some intensively negative attachment to the other." Most of these leaders had a close relationship with their mothers, who appeared to favor them over other siblings. Sigmund Freud made a similar observation when, in *The Interpretation of Dreams*, he wrote, "I have found that people who know that they are preferred or favoured by their mother[s] give evidence in their lives of a peculiar self-reliance and an unshakable optimism which often seem like heroic attributes and bring actual success to their possessors."

Abraham Lincoln, similarly, had a very close bond with his stepmother, Sarah Bush Johnston Lincoln. She was a constant source of encouragement and love to her stepson. Mrs. Lincoln considered Abraham "a model child who never needed a cross word." She recalled that her mind and his "seemed to run together." Lincoln spoke only in kindness of Sarah Lincoln and always called her "mother." In later years, he provided for her, in part, by keeping the forty acres of land on which she lived in his name.

He visited her for the last time in early 1861, just before he left for Washington to take the oath of office. They embraced, cried, held hands, and talked most of the day. To friends who accompanied him, Lincoln spoke very affectionately of his stepmother, calling her the best friend he'd ever had and recalling the positive change she'd brought about in his life. This last visit in itself says much about the attachment they shared. Here was Lincoln, off to face a task even "greater than that which rested upon Washington," taking time to visit his mother, his earliest and strongest source of reassurance and support.

By contrast, there was a major estrangement between Lincoln and his father. Thomas Lincoln "grew up literally without education," as Lincoln would later write, and "he never did more in the way of writing than to bunglingly sign his own name."

Abraham, however, was more given to intellectual pursuits, which may have been the chief cause for a lack of bonding and affection between the two. The boy took it upon himself to learn to read and write, and then subsequently expanded his abilities by leaps and bounds. A perfect example of the depth of the rift between the two is that Lincoln did not attend his father's funeral. When he received word that Thomas was near death, Lincoln wrote to his stepbrother, John D. Johnston: "Say to him that if we could meet now, it is doubtful whether it would not be more painful than pleasant. . . ."

In addition to the complex relationship many distinguished leaders have had with their parents, Burns notes several other similarities. Many experienced some form of tragedy while still very young. Lenin, Hitler, and Gandhi all lost their fathers at an early age. Some were forced to accept the mutual tolerance of others while growing up (such as Gandhi, who lived with his parents, brothers and sisters, and five uncles and their families). Virtually all of the outstanding leaders Burns studied were "subject to feelings of insecurity and lack of self-esteem." Moreover, most developed a dynamic will to succeed, a driving ambition that lasted their entire lives.

Compare this profile with that of Abraham Lincoln: His mother died when he was nine years old. His sister, Sarah, died in childbirth when he was nineteen. After his father remarried a woman with three children, Abraham was forced to live in a small log cabin with seven other people. As a youth, he was so gangly and gawky-looking that he was teased unmercifully by young girls; through his adolescence and into adulthood, he masked his shyness by acting the clown and telling funny stories.

The life of Abraham Lincoln, especially his presidency, demonstrated that he possessed all of the great leadership qualities. Some of his inherent abilities were natural; others were consciously developed over the course of his life. Qualities such as honesty and integrity, empathy for the common man, and devotion to the rights of individuals were products of his upbringing. During his adult life, Lincoln's chosen profession as a lawyer prepared him for his future executive leadership position. He learned to express himself and demonstrate to others his beliefs and thoughts. Most importantly, he refined his ability to persuade, direct, and motivate people. In running for public office Lincoln became an excellent orator and speech writer. In fact, he so dramatically increased his ability to speak and write that he is today regarded as a model for poetic and artistic expression.

Lincoln combined an extraordinary wit with a gift for storytelling to become an effective communicator. He was naturally inquisitive and he learned rapidly, which led him to be extremely innovative. He is, in fact, the only U.S. president to hold a patent (for a method to make grounded boats more buoyant). He had a "penetrating and far-reaching" voice that could be heard over great distances. For example, everyone present heard the entire Gettysburg Address, and there were at least 15,000 people in attendance. Even Lincoln's height (at six feet, four inches, our tallest president) gave him a psychological advantage over others. He was a man to be looked up to, a man to be followed.

Assessing the accomplishments of Abraham Lincoln as president of the United States confirms that he must have been an excellent leader. How else could the Union Government have worked cohesively to win the Civil War and keep the country together in so relatively brief a time frame? What makes this accomplishment even more remarkable is that he was able to overcome the nightmare he inherited from outgoing President James Buchanan.

By the time Lincoln took office, seven states had seceded from the Union to form the Confederate States of America. Barely ten days before he took the oath of office on March 4, 1861, Jefferson Davis was sworn in as president of the Confederacy in Montgomery, Alabama. President Buchanan had given up hope of holding the country together and was simply waiting for his term to expire. Moreover, Buchanan left Washington proclaiming that he was "the last President of the United States."

Nor had the United States Congress taken any action whatsoever to put down the rebellion. In fact, while a bill was tabled in the House of Representatives that would have given the president power to call out the state militias, the Senate passed a resolution requesting the War Department to lower military spending. All this happened between the time Lincoln was elected and the time he took office. When he finally became president, Lincoln was faced with the realization that the South had taken control of all federal agencies and had seized almost every fort and arsenal in Southern territory. Most of the Mississippi River, lifeblood of the nation's commerce and trade, was obstructed or in Southern hands. Washington was left almost completely defenseless, protected only by a portion of the nation's army, which in 1861 was unprepared for war. It was a scattered, dilapidated, poorly equipped, and disorganized array of some 16,000 soldiers, many of them Southern sympathizers. In charge was General Winfield Scott, who was viewed by many as incompetent. In addition, most of the state militias were in much worse shape than the federal army.

Rumors persisted that Lincoln's inauguration was to be disrupted, the president killed, and the city taken by the Confederates. The nation's capital was placed under armed alert. When Lincoln delivered his First Inaugural Address, the nation was in a crisis more severe and ominous than at any other time in American history. The country was divided, hatred was the most prevalent emotion, and there was no effective leadership anywhere in the government.

In the midst of all this turmoil, the relatively unknown Abraham Lincoln took the oath as the nation's sixteenth president. The first Republican president, elected by a minority of the popular vote, he was a Washington outsider who was viewed widely as a second-rate country lawyer and completely ill-equipped and unable to handle the presidency. He commanded no respect from anyone in the nation except his most loyal supporters. Even the members of his newly appointed cabinet considered him a figurehead whom they could control. Politically, Lincoln was caught between the fierce abolitionists of the Northern states and the slaveholders of the border states that he desperately wanted to remain in the Union. Holding onto states such as Kentucky and Maryland was crucial to the preservation of the nation he had just sworn to preserve, protect, and defend. Yet, he was pressured constantly to free the slaves. Not that he was for slavery, for he believed that "if slavery is not wrong, nothing is wrong," but the timing was not right to grant emancipation. To do so at such an early stage of his presidency would only serve to further divide the country. He correctly concluded that some, if not all, of the border states would secede were he to call for the complete abolition of slavery.

Lincoln, therefore, was faced with the seemingly insurmountable problem of holding the nation together while at the same time organizing a new, more effective government that could prepare for an impending civil war. In his Inaugural Address he had declared that the Southern states would not be allowed to separate and that the "momentous issue of civil war" was in their hands. Yet he had no means at his disposal to keep them in the Union. That he knew exactly what he was up against is evident from his own words early in the address:

> It is seventy-two years since the first inauguration of a President under our national Constitution. . . . I

now enter upon the . . . task for the brief constitutional term of four years, under great and peculiar difficulty. A disruption of the Federal Union, heretofore only menaced, is now formidably attempted.

Such was the situation for a man who'd never before held an executive leadership position; who had been only a one-term national congressman; who had had no military experience to speak of, had never been in battle, and indeed had been only an elected captain in the Illinois militia briefly during the Black Hawk War. Abraham Lincoln appeared unable to lead the nation out of its dark dilemma. Few people at the time could have known, however, that he possessed all the leadership qualities and abilities necessary to save the Union. And virtually no one would have been able to predict the unparalleled strength of his leadership—that he would seize upon the very circumstances at hand, created by the crises of confusion, urgency, and desperation, to exercise the full power of his office, and to create *new* limits of authority and leadership for the presidency.

Why would today's leaders be interested in Abraham Lincoln's leadership style and philosophy? Because, by modern standards, Lincoln's accomplishment would be regarded as no less than a miracle. There can be no doubt that Lincoln is the greatest leader this country, and perhaps this world, has yet known. He literally towers over such modern day exemplars as Iacocca, Reagan, or Bush. There is no real comparison.

Lincoln was the man who really knew how to lead.

Lincoln is the leader who genuinely has something new to offer contemporary business and political leaders.

And here are his lessons and principles.

PART I
PEOPLE

> His cardinal mistake is that he isolates himself, & allows nobody to see him; and by which he does not know what is going on in the very matter he is dealing with.

> Lincoln's reason for relieving Gen. John C. Fremont from his command in Missouri (September 9, 1861)

1 / *Get Out of the Office and Circulate Among the Troops*

During his four years as president Abraham Lincoln spent most of his time among the troops. They were number one to him; they were the people who were going to get the job done. He virtually lived at the War Department's telegraph office so he could gain access to key information for quick, timely decisions. He met with his generals and cabinet members in their homes, offices, and in the field, principally to provide direction and leadership. He toured the Navy Yard and the fortifications in and around Washington, and inspected new weaponry, all to obtain accurate knowledge of the workings and abilities of the armed forces. This contact also gave him the first-hand knowledge he needed to make informed, accurate decisions without having to rely solely on the word of others. He visited other key individuals in the government, such as members of Congress, and toured hospitals to visit the sick and wounded, which demonstrated his compassionate and caring nature. Lincoln even went to the field to observe or take charge of several battle situations himself, coming under fire at least once (one of the few American presidents to do so while in office).

On October 24, 1861, Lincoln relieved Gen. John C. Fremont from command of the Department of the West (headquartered in Missouri) and replaced him with Gen. David Hunter. Among other things, Fremont had issued a proclamation (promptly revoked by Lincoln) declaring martial law and ordering slaves freed in his jurisdiction. Fremont had also misused public funds and surrounded himself with unethical advisers, and he was completely out of touch with those he commanded and the situation at hand. He turned out to be a terribly inept leader. In a letter to General Hunter, written shortly before relieving Fremont, Lincoln summarized his view of the situation. "He [General Fremont] is losing the confidence of men near him, whose support any man in his position must have to be successful," said Lincoln. "His cardinal mistake is that he isolates himself, and allows nobody to see him; and by which he does not know what is going on in the very matter he is dealing with."

Lincoln's letter is something of a lesson in itself for today's leaders. Not only did he explain his problem with Fremont in writing; he also offered Hunter advice on how to solve the problem and avoid making the same "cardinal mistake." General Hunter could now have no misconceptions about what Lincoln demanded of him as Fremont's replacement. Further, with this letter Lincoln revealed the cornerstone of his own personal leadership philosophy, an approach that would become part of a revolution in modern leadership thinking 100 years later when it was dubbed MBWA (Managing by Wandering Around) by Tom Peters and Robert Waterman in their 1982 book *In Search of Excellence*. It has been referred to by other names and phrases, such as: "roving leadership," "being in touch," or "getting out of the ivory tower." Whatever the label, it's simply the process of stepping out and interacting with people, of establishing *human contact*.

Peters and Nancy Austin, in *A Passion For Excellence*, define MBWA as "the technology of the obvious":

> It is being in touch, with customers, suppliers, your people. It facilitates innovation, and makes possible the teaching of values to every member of an organization. Listening, facilitating, and teaching and reinforcing values. What is this except leadership? Thus, MBWA is the technology of leadership. Leading is primarily paying attention. The masters of the use of attention are also not only master users of symbols, of drama, but master storytellers and myth builders.

For all they knew, Peters and Austin could have been describing not only the very methods employed by Abraham Lincoln but Lincoln himself: master user of symbols and drama, and master storyteller and myth builder.

Lincoln was a natural wanderer. As a lawyer in Springfield, Illinois, he spent a great deal of time away from home, not only riding the circuit, but also seeking facts and information pertinent to any case he may have been working on at the time. He was the kind of lawyer who would go out and discover firsthand what was going on. This was one of the major elements that made him so successful at his profession. Nothing is so powerful (or frustrating to the opposition) as an attorney who knows the facts, and Lincoln made it a point to always have the key information at hand. The same principle holds for a good leader. Lincoln carried this approach over to the presidency. His curiosity, combined with his new station as a Washington outsider, may have led him to be even more inquisitive than normal after taking the oath of office. Lincoln realized that people were a major source of information and that to be a good leader he had to stay close to them. Without question, Lincoln's visibility and open-door policy as president constitute an exemplary model for effective leadership.

His basic philosophy was that he would see as many people as often as he possibly could. John Nicolay and John Hay, his personal secretaries, reported that Lincoln spent 75 percent of his time meeting with people. No matter how busy the president was, he always seemed to find time for those who called on him. To this extent, he ran the White House much as he had run his law office in Springfield, where the door was always open and anyone who wished to come in and talk was welcome. Often Nicolay or Hay would tell a visitor that the president was busy and they should come back later, whereupon Lincoln would open his office door and welcome the visitor anyway.

President Lincoln would not maintain any distance between himself and the people, which made it difficult to guard him. He frequently complained about all the well-meaning protection: "It is important that the people know I come among them without fear," he would declare and then proceed to elude his military guard or order them back to the War Department. Lincoln would not become a prisoner in his own office. He maintained a flexibility that was unusual for chief executives of the time. Often he'd ignore presidential etiquette and burst in on one of his cabinet members while they were conducting a meeting. He'd also convene cabinet meetings at odd places such as the Navy Yard or in the War Department. Moreover, Lincoln would not wait for his cabinet to come to him on their regularly scheduled Tuesday and Friday noon meetings but preferred instead to meet with the members on an individual basis, usually in the secretary's office.

For Lincoln, casual contact with his subordinates was as important as formal gatherings, if not more so, and today's leaders should take note of this style. He preferred, whenever possible, to interact with people when they were in a more relaxed, less pressure-packed environment.

The most frequently visited cabinet member was Secretary of War Edwin M. Stanton. Nearly every day Lincoln walked from the White House to Stanton's office at the War Department about a block away. Sometimes during critical battles Lincoln made the trek two or three times a day, and once in a while he even spent the night in the telegraph office waiting for dispatches from the field.

Vivid pictures of Lincoln have been re-created from the recollections of men who observed him during critical parts of the war. For example, during the first battle of the Seven Days, where Robert E. Lee surprised and attacked George McClellan's troops, Gen. John Pope recalled the president spending many hours on Stanton's sofa waiting for news and looking depressed and anxious. During the Wilderness campaign, when news from the field was impossible to obtain, Lincoln was spotted drifting from office to office gathering information and asking people if they had heard any rumors about General Grant. And there are numerous reports of Lincoln spending all night at the War Department monitoring the plans and strategic details of major operations.

This type of hands-on, personal approach was typical of Lincoln's leadership style. However, when he couldn't get out of the White House, he let people "wander" to him. In fact, Lincoln was probably the most accessible chief executive the United States has ever known. Government officials, businessmen, and ordinary citizens literally lined the walls of the Executive Mansion in the hope of getting in to see him. Lincoln turned away very few people, and some he even encouraged to visit. To a man in Indiana, Lincoln wrote in 1863, "I do not often decline seeing people who call upon me; and probably will see you if you call."

He made himself accessible to the people as often as the responsibilities of his job permitted. "I tell you," he once said, "that I call these receptions my 'public opinion baths'—for I have little time to read the papers and gather public opinion that way; and though they may not be pleasant in all particulars, the effect, as a whole, is renovating and invigorating."

This almost startling access to the president, created by

Lincoln himself, brings up another important principle for modern leaders. If subordinates, or people in general, know that they genuinely have easy access to their leader, they'll tend to view the leader in a more positive, trustworthy light. "Hey," the followers think, "this guy really wants to hear from me—to know what I think and what's really going on. He *must* be committed to making things work!" And so Lincoln was.

Through all of his public opinion baths and his wandering from office to office, there is one key element that shouldn't be overlooked in Lincoln's style, and that was his amiability. "All [who] claim the personal acquaintance of Mr. Lincoln," wrote one newspaperman of the day, "will agree that he is the very embodiment of good temper and affability. They will all concede that he has a kind word, an encouraging smile, a humorous remark for nearly all [who seek] his presence, and that but few, if any, emerge from his reception room without being strongly and favorably impressed with his general disposition."

A positive outlook and a pleasant disposition can yield valuable dividends for any leader, and Lincoln knew it. "Everyone likes a compliment," wrote Lincoln to Thurlow Weed in 1865. He knew that people like to be complimented, that they enjoy sincere praise as well as talking and hearing about themselves. As always, he put his knowledge to good use. As a lawyer in Springfield the effect of his compliments on others provided a powerful motivational force in getting things accomplished. As president, it worked even better. After a young man asked Lincoln to autograph a photograph and commented that he must be annoyed frequently by such requests, Lincoln is reported to have replied: "Well, I suppose you know that men will stand a good deal when they are flattered." It's a good lesson to remember. Affability, flattery, and a pleasant demeanor go hand in hand with human contact, not only because people tend to "stand a good deal," as Lincoln put it, but also because it allows them to be more relaxed, at ease, and open with their thoughts and feelings.

President George Bush has enjoyed a solid reputation for being a pleasant, amiable person. Yet, early in his administration he was criticized for spending too much time away from Washington. He was accused of running a "helter-skelter" presidency, and many of his critics wondered, aloud and in print, if he was allergic to the White House. But whether Bush realizes it or not, he has ample precedent for his excursions.

As remarkable as it may seem, in 1861 Lincoln spent more time *out* of the White House than he did in it. And the chances are good that if a Union soldier had enlisted early in the Civil War, he saw the president in person. Lincoln made it a point to personally inspect every state regiment of volunteers that passed through Washington, D.C., on their way to the front; and early in the war, they all passed through Washington. Lincoln would inspect the troops where they were encamped on the banks of the Potomac River, or he'd salute them from a balcony at the Willard Hotel as they marched through the streets. On one rainy day, later in the war, Lincoln got drenched while he stood on that same balcony as the soldiers cheered him enthusiastically. "If they can stand it," he said, "I guess I can." He'd also review the troops on the Capitol or White House grounds, in neighboring Virginia or Maryland, or he would simply speak to them as they stopped by the White House to serenade him. Wherever the soldiers were, there would be Lincoln. "He goes at it with both hands," the *New York Times* once reported, "and hand over hand . . . gives [a] good honest hearty shake, as if he meant it."

This type of personal contact helped Lincoln show the troops that the government appreciated their efforts. Throughout the war Lincoln continued to visit his generals and men in the field. Often he'd ride his horse along the lines of troops, waving his stovepipe hat as the men cheered wildly. In addition, he always had a kind word for them, frequently telling them his vision of America and how important they were in achieving victory in the cause for which they were fighting. It was they who rendered "the hardest work in support of the government," he'd say. It was they who "should be given the greatest credit."

Lincoln also made it a point to visit hospitals where wounded soldiers were recuperating. After the first battle of Bull Run, for example, the president visited the wounded in and around Washington several times, accompanied by Mrs. Lincoln or Secretary of State Seward. In 1862, he called on Lieutenant Worden, commander of the *Monitor*, who was nearly blinded by a shell in the famous battle with the *Merrimac*. During this meeting he "burst into tears while greeting the sailor," most likely because he was still in an emotional state since the death of his son, Willie, just a few weeks earlier.

Lincoln often attended private funerals, whether it was for the infant son of his secretary of war (Edwin M. Stanton) or for eighteen women killed in an explosion at the federal arsenal. During his presidency, Lincoln visited the wounded in hospitals and private residences and attended funerals any time such an occasion presented itself. This striking visible display of compassion and caring on the part of the president inspired trust, loyalty, and admiration not just from the soldiers but also from his subordinates.

Lincoln also called on Congress regularly. In fact, he was the first sitting president in more than twenty-five years to attend a regular working session of the Senate. He knew he needed the help of congressmen and senators to win the war effort, and what better way to begin to gain their support than to be visible? So, he established contact with them—human contact. And throughout his presidency, Lincoln continued to visit Congress periodically. Lincoln would work with Congress if they supported his efforts. He would not, however, tolerate delay or inaction. He was the commander-in-chief and would direct and lead the armed forces and the government. Congress would not deter his quest to preserve the Union.

In order to make timely and reliable decisions Lincoln needed access to information. Basically, he relied on three major sources: reports from trusted confidants and advisers; his practice of going to the field; and the modern communication technology of the age, the telegraph.

Rather than haunting the War Department's Telegraph Office, Lincoln could have waited in the White House for a messenger to bring him word of progress in key battles. But he preferred to be right there, peering over the shoulder of the decoder and getting the information as fast as it came in. This put Lincoln in a position where he could make quick decisions with virtually no delay. Upon receiving updates from his generals the president could compose a telegram and then hand it to the nearest messenger to relay his orders to the battlefield. There is no question that Lincoln's style was effective, nor is there any question that he won battles and saved countless lives by acting swiftly and decisively.

All leaders must seek and require access to reliable and up-to-date information. And Lincoln was constantly seeking key intelligence so he could make quick, timely, and effective decisions. He needed accurate information, and the best way to obtain it was to go out and get it himself. Also, for a leader, there is a certain amount of value and effect in seeing people outside of the everyday business environment or out of the leader's office. In an informal setting people tend to be more relaxed, more direct, more truthful than if they were face to face in the Oval Office. That's what Lincoln wanted—honest talk with people. He needed to know the truth. And Abraham Lincoln had an innate ability to perceive the truth. He could receive information unbiased by filters and prejudices, process it, and then communicate it in the common man's vernacular so that everyone could understand.

For Lincoln, the best way to assess a situation was to collect data personally. But there were times when he needed information and couldn't find the time to get away. That's when he would send trusted advisers to gather the facts and report back to him. Time after time Lincoln used this method of gathering the evidence he needed to take appropriate action. For instance, during the crisis at Fort Sumter, Lincoln was besieged with advice on how to handle the situation. Gen. Winfield Scott and Secretary of State William H. Seward wanted to surrender the fort; others in his inner circle wanted to hold Sumter at all costs. The president was torn on the issue of whether to reinforce or resupply, alternatives that both seemed to mean full-scale war. To make the correct decision, Lincoln sent one of his trusted colleagues, Stephen A. Hurlbut, on a fact-finding mission to Charleston. He was to meet with the Confederate leaders, evaluate the situation, and report back within a few weeks. When Hurlbut returned to Washington with a written report for the president, it was clear to Lincoln the course he must take. War, according to Hurlbut, was inevitable unless the South was allowed to secede. Lincoln decided to resupply the embattled fort; if his ships were fired upon, it would be the Confederacy that started the war, not the Union.

Repeatedly, Lincoln would dispatch one of his cabinet members or military officers to an area that needed a decision from him. Such was the case when he sent Postmaster General Montgomery Blair and Quartermaster Montgomery Meigs to Missouri to investigate General Fremont's "cardinal mistake." In addition, it was not uncommon for Lincoln to summon witnesses from major battles to the White House so he could have firsthand accounts. Henry Stoddard, who had helped with the wounded after the second battle of Bull Run (1862), described what he saw and heard to the president. Gen. Herman Haupt rushed from the battlefield at Gettysburg in July 1863 to confer with Lincoln; in 1864, H. E. Wing arrived in the early morning hours aboard a special train to give the president an eyewitness account of the Wilderness campaign.

Lincoln's roving leadership style is illustrated in Figure 1, which graphs the total number of days per month he was, in part, out of the office. In 1861, during the early stages of his presidency and the Civil War, he was active nearly the entire year. He had to find out what was going on, determine the lay

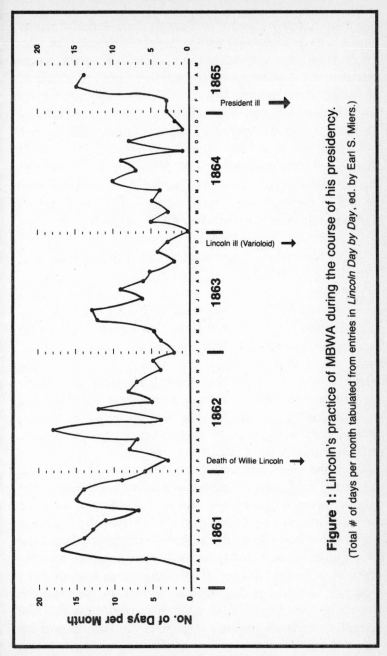

Figure 1: Lincoln's practice of MBWA during the course of his presidency.

(Total # of days per month tabulated from entries in *Lincoln Day by Day*, ed. by Earl S. Miers.)

of the land, and get to know his people. There were many decisions to be made that first year. In the subsequent years (1862–1864), Lincoln was in the field frequently, with peaks of activity in the warm spring and summer months and lows in the colder winter months. Two of the lowest points during his tenure as president occurred in February 1862, when his son, Willie, died; and in December 1863 and January 1864, when he was ill and recovering from varioloid (a mild form of smallpox). Other than that, it was difficult to keep Abraham Lincoln *in* the White House. As a matter of fact, in 1865, with the end of the war near, Lincoln spent half of the month of March and the first fourteen days of April doing little else than visiting his troops in the field. He had seen before what he felt could have been final victory snatched away or lost because of inactivity or lack of follow-up. This time he would take charge, see for himself, and make certain the war would come to a swift conclusion. This tremendous burst of activity on Lincoln's part toward the war's end, coupled with his high output early in the conflict, demonstrated that he was a "hands-on" leader. He was there when it counted—decisively taking charge, as well as influencing, guiding, teaching, and directing. And Lincoln also was learning from others. He was doing what all leaders should do. He was acquiring new skills gleaned from his followers through frequent personal contact. Lincoln was learning while on the job.

When the Civil War finally ended, President Lincoln was still in the field, returning from a trip that took him to the recently captured Confederate capital of Richmond, where he toured the city and sat in Jefferson Davis's chair and heard the troops break into cheers. Arriving in Washington aboard the *River Queen* in the evening hours of April 9, 1865, Lincoln was one of the last people in Washington to hear of Lee's surrender to Grant at Appomattox. Typical of the man, the first thing that Lincoln did upon his arrival was to head straight to William Seward's residence. He had to visit his friend, the secretary of state who, while Lincoln was gone, had suffered an accident and was bedridden.

Future leaders can learn from Lincoln's example. One of the most effective ways to gain acceptance of a philosophy is to show it in your daily actions. In order to stage your leadership style, you must have an audience. By entering your subordinate's environment—by establishing frequent human contact—you create a sense of commitment, collaboration, and community. You also gain access to vital information necessary to make effective decisions. Additionally, when personal contact is not possible, you can send surrogates to the field to obtain information.

Many leaders in today's complex work settings would argue that they can't spend the amount of time Lincoln did with his subordinates. But, then again, they're not trying to win a war. Or are they?

LINCOLN PRINCIPLES

★ Explain yourself in writing and offer advice on how to solve problems.

★ It is important that the people know you come among them without fear.

★ Seek casual contact with your subordinates. It is as meaningful as a formal gathering, if not more so.

★ Don't often decline to see people who call on you.

★ Take public opinion baths.

★ Be the very embodiment of good temper and affability.

★ Remember, everyone likes a compliment.

★ If your subordinates can stand it, so can you. Set a good example.

★ You must seek and require access to reliable and up-to-date information.

A house divided against itself cannot stand. . . . Our cause must be intrusted to, and conducted by its own undoubted friends—whose hands are free, whose hearts are in the work—who *do care* for the result.

Lincoln's remarks from "A House Divided" speech, in which he accepted the nomination for U.S. senator at the Republican State Convention in Springfield, Illinois (June 16, 1858)

2 / *Build Strong Alliances*

Abraham Lincoln gained the trust and respect of his subordinates, building strong alliances on both personal and professional levels. He wanted to know how his people would respond in any given situation: who would have a tendency to get the job done on his own, or be more likely to procrastinate and delay; who could be counted on in an emergency and who couldn't; who were the brighter, more able, more committed people; who shared his strong sense of ethics and values. He also wanted his subordinates to get to know him, so that they would know how *he* would respond in any given situation, what he wanted, demanded, and needed. If they knew what *he* would do, they could make their own decisions without asking him for direction, thereby avoiding delay and inactivity.

Recent studies in the field of leadership recognize and stress the need for building strong interpersonal relationships and bonds. In their book *Leaders*, Warren Bennis and Burt Nanus note that "leadership establishes trust" and "leaders pay attention"; they observe that leaders "have the ability to trust others even if the risk seems great." Peters and Austin put it more bluntly by simply stating that "attention is all there is" and that "trust is learned only by example." The power of effective listening has also gained a great deal of attention. Lee Iacocca, Chrysler's leader, writes in his autobiography: "I only wish I could find an institute that teaches people how to listen. After all, a good manager needs to *listen* at least as much as he needs to talk. Too many people fail to realize that real communication goes in both directions."

Abraham Lincoln listened, paid attention, and established trust. He worked hard at forging strong relationships with all of his subordinates, especially the members of his cabinet and his commanding generals. In some cases the president overcame intense negative feelings toward him on the part of a few individuals. For example, William H. Seward, Lincoln's secretary of state, initially thought the president to be well-intentioned yet totally unqualified and incompetent to run the administration and lead the country. There was also some personal animosity involved because Seward had been the front-runner for the 1860 Republican presidential nomination, which, of course, went to the less well known, more middle-of-the-road candidate Abraham Lincoln. After accepting the offer to become secretary of state, Seward attempted to influence Lincoln's selections for the rest of the cabinet. However, he found the president-elect to be firm and resourceful, with a distinct mind of his own. He became so frustrated in his efforts to change Lincoln's mind that he submitted his resignation even before the inauguration. But, immediately after taking the oath, Lincoln met with Seward and, appealing to his patriotic duty and sense of self-worth, persuaded him to stay on.

In the early months of the new administration, Seward attempted to lead the war effort and direct the cabinet himself. But again he found Lincoln to be much stronger than he'd envisioned at first. When Seward undertook private and secret negotiations with the South, assuring its leaders that Fort Sumter would be evacuated, Lincoln overruled him by deciding to resupply the fort. The overzealous secretary of state then sent the president a chastising memorandum that outlined what he felt the policy should be toward the South. He even suggested that the United States instigate a war with a foreign country to unify the nation against a common enemy. Lincoln promptly responded with a letter of his own, the substance of which was probably also delivered to Seward orally. If such policies were to be instituted, "*I* must do it," said Lincoln. Seward found out immediately that the new president could be tough and decisive. Undaunted, later in 1861 he attempted to push Lincoln into a conflict with England after the British vessel *Trent* was captured with two Confederate commissioners on board. Again, Lincoln held firm. "One war at a time," he cautioned Seward.

Despite all this early turmoil and difference of opinion, Seward and Lincoln soon became allies. The president would stop by the secretary's home for long visits during which the two men would take turns telling funny stories and anecdotes. They also would take carriage rides together in and around Washington, often viewing the troops and fortifications. After they got to know each other, it turned out that they had similar political views. They shared a deep commitment to the nation, a strong penchant for common sense, and high ethics and values. Soon Seward was making numerous suggestions for Lincoln's speeches and proclamations. And Lincoln was inclined to interfere very little in foreign affairs, preferring instead to delegate that responsibility and authority to the secretary of state. In a very short period of time Seward had turned from an attitude of skepticism and mistrust toward Lincoln to one of loyalty and admiration. "Executive force and vigor are rare qualities," Seward wrote to his wife in 1861. "The President is the best of us."

Interestingly enough, the two men to whom Lincoln became the closest were also the two who had originally thought the worst of him. They were also the two most competent and able men in the cabinet. The first was Seward; the other was Lincoln's second secretary of war, Edwin M. Stanton, who first met the future president in 1855 when both were involved in the McCormick Reaper case. Stanton, at the time a renowned attorney, evidently insulted the less well known Lincoln (reportedly calling him a giraffe). He apparently felt the same way after Lincoln's rise to power, believing that the president had "no token of any intelligent understanding."

Despite all of the negative feelings displayed by Stanton, Lincoln still appointed him the new secretary of war because he knew he was the best man for the job. Stanton accepted the job enthusiastically and quickly proved Lincoln correct in his judgment. In a few months Stanton thoroughly revamped the War Department into an efficient organization. He worked long exhausting hours in a tireless effort to serve his country and win the war.

Early in the administration, Stanton was friends with Gen. George McClellan, and both had intense scorn for Lincoln. However, as time passed (and after he became secretary of war), Stanton grew to dislike McClellan's delay tactics and began to appreciate Lincoln's quest for action and victory. He also supported men like Grant who fought and posted victories. Lincoln, Stanton began to think, was not the buffoon he originally believed him to be. Lincoln, in turn, came to respect, admire, and understand Stanton. He realized that under a somewhat surly exterior existed an honest, devoted, and thoroughly capable administrator. As a result, he let Stanton run the War Department as he saw fit. Often Lincoln would sign stack after stack of military commissions that he did not bother to read. He looked only for his secretary of war's signature, thinking that if Stanton had approved them they must be alright. The two men became so close that when Lincoln arrived back in Washington aboard the *River Queen* early in the evening of April 9, 1865, it was Stanton who (with a bear hug) greeted him with the news of Lee's surrender at Appomattox. And, when Lincoln died, it was Stanton who is reported to have muttered, "Now he belongs to the ages." The president's son, Robert, also later recalled how Stanton "for more than ten days after my father's death in Washington, called every morning on me in my room, and spent the first few minutes of his visits weeping without saying a word."

Today's leaders can learn a thing or two from Lincoln's relationship with Seward and Stanton. Simply spending time together and getting to know one's subordinates can overcome mountains of personal differences and hard feelings. If followers learn that their leader is firm, resolute, and committed in the daily performance of his duty, respect can be gained, and trust will soon follow. Lincoln's approach won't work for everyone. Some employees simply will not come around. However, the vast majority—the most competent and honest ones—will. And should there be too many of those who don't see the merit in this approach, they could perhaps be construed to be in the wrong place.

For all the successful relationships Lincoln had with key subordinates, he, too, had his share of failures. One notable problem manifested itself in the form of Gen. George Brinton McClellan, the "Young Napoleon." Upon the retirement of Gen. Winfield Scott (which Lincoln orchestrated), the president appointed McClellan general-in-chief. Even though the general had displayed a tendency toward inaction as commander of the Army of the Potomac, Lincoln admired the young man's confidence and his ability to organize and train the troops. He was also very popular with his soldiers, a fact that Lincoln viewed with approval.

On the evening of November 1, 1861, the day he appointed McClellan general-in-chief, President Lincoln visited the general at his residence to give him fatherly advice about the responsibilities of his new position. "In addition to your present command, the supreme command of the Army will entail a vast labor upon you," he counseled. "I can do it all," assured McClellan. But Lincoln was not so sure that he could. And now that the young general was supreme commander he saw a lot more of the president than he had previously. Not only was Lincoln there the first day he appointed McClellan to his new post, but he also visited him, either at his headquarters or residence, nearly every day for the next few weeks. Often Lincoln would wander into the general's office and make small talk or tell an amusing story. The president made McClellan feel important by going to him more often than he summoned the general to the White House. At many of these conferences the president listened, discussed, and in some cases directed a broad approach and strategy, but he always left it up to General McClellan to perform the task at hand. Lincoln used these meetings to assess the general and to let McClellan get to know him. After a time, however, McClellan began to dislike what he viewed as Lincoln's meddling. He failed to realize what the president was trying to do. After one short discussion in which Lincoln apparently made a few operational suggestions, McClellan remarked to a key officer: "Isn't he a rare bird?"

After months of maintaining a defensive posture, McClellan made it apparent he was not going to act on his own. So the president was forced to give more direction. When he did, McClellan's attitude turned abrasive and disrespectful. One of the general's more remarkable snubs of the president occurred on the night of November 13, 1861, when Lincoln, Seward, and John Hay called at McClellan's house. A servant, while ushering the trio into the parlor, informed the president that McClellan was at a wedding and would soon return. About an hour later the general came back and, upon being informed that Lincoln was waiting to see him, marched past the parlor and went upstairs to bed. Hay and Seward were outraged, but Lincoln seemed to be less affected, remarking to the younger Hay that it was "better at this time not to be making points of etiquette and personal dignity." Privately, however, he must have been disturbed by the episode because it was now evident that McClellan had mistaken Lincoln's visits to him as a sign of weakness rather than one of strength and resourcefulness. It is also significant to note that thereafter President Lincoln began summoning McClellan to the Executive Mansion rather than going to the general.

During the course of their relationship, Lincoln treated McClellan with the same respect and dignity that he offered to Stanton and Seward. Lincoln did get to know McClellan, and McClellan Lincoln. Their alliance, however, had many highs and lows, was inconsistent, and troubled Lincoln deeply. Even though the president supported and defended his general to complaining congressmen and senators, McClellan seemed incapable of taking the field. McClellan, however, genuinely appreciated the president's support, for on February 22, 1862 (only a few days after Lincoln's son died), the general wrote consolingly to him: "You have been a kind true friend to me . . . during the last few months. Your confidence has upheld me when I should otherwise have felt weak."

Lincoln eventually was forced to remove McClellan from command and later found the former general to be his opponent in the presidential election of 1864. His rift with the president having gained the attention of the press, McClellan was able to secure the Democratic presidential nomination, only to be soundly defeated at the polls.

It hurt Lincoln somewhat not to have formed a successful link with McClellan, but at least he'd maintained his own integrity. The lesson to be learned here is to simply not give up attempting to build solid alliances. For every failed attempt like the relationship with McClellan, there may be two successful ones like Seward and Stanton.

And even though his personal relationship with George McClellan was troubled, Lincoln did ally successfully with most of his generals. If they didn't like the constant changes in command he made, they respected his decisions. Gen. Ambrose Burnside once remarked in 1862 to his staff: "If ever there was an honest man on the face of the earth it was

Abraham Lincoln." And when Gen. William S. Rosecrans was approached by some radical Republicans to run against Lincoln for the nomination of 1864, he responded that they were wrong to oppose Lincoln. "He's in the right place," admonished the general. Even Ulysses S. Grant refused to run for president as long as Lincoln wanted the job.

Lincoln gained commitment and respect from his people because he was willing to take time out from his busy schedule to hear what his people had to say. It's no different when you're running a business. If you stay in touch with the people who comprise the foundation, you're more likely to gain an advantage that helps you to win the war against stiff competition. It's the people who are closest to the consumer and the product who know how to win. And, almost always, they will want to offer their ideas.

Lincoln's success in forging alliances could be attributed, in part, to his deep understanding of human nature. "Plain common sense, a kindly disposition, a straight forward purpose, and a shrewd perception of the ins and outs of poor, weak human nature," noted the *New York Herald* in 1864, "have enabled him to master difficulties which would have swamped any other man." It was this penetrating comprehension of human nature that helped Lincoln possess the compassion necessary to issue the many pardons, for which he is so famous, to deserting soldiers during the Civil War. In 1863 he noted:

> Actual war coming, blood grows hot, and blood is spilled. Thought is forced from old channels into confusion. Deception breeds and thrives. Confidence dies, and universal suspicion reigns. Each man feels an impulse to kill his neighbor, lest he be first killed by him. Revenge and retaliation follow. And all this, as before said, may be among honest men only.

Lincoln understood the motives of men and how they tended to react under stress. As a result, he was very lenient of what was perceived by many to be cowardly conduct. The plain fact that Lincoln granted so many pardons just naturally helped him build successful affiliations with his followers. Not that he granted pardons as a strategy for alliance-building. It was done, rather, because Lincoln was a kind and caring human being. But people are much more likely to trust a leader if they know he is compassionate and forgiving of mistakes. And *trust*, of course, is the essential building block for successful relationships.

The ability to understand human nature helped Lincoln deal with nations as well as individuals. In 1861, for example, when Great Britain and the United States were squabbling over the capture of the British vessel *Trent* with two Confederate commissioners aboard, many of the president's advisers were concerned about the possibility of a more serious conflict— perhaps even war. But Lincoln, with one of his characteristic stories, revealed a much more intuitive understanding of the reality of the situation when he said:

> I remember when I was a lad, there were two fields behind our house separated by a fence. In each field there was a big bulldog, and these dogs spent the whole day racing up and down, snarling and yelping at each other through that fence. One day they both came at the same moment to a hole in it, big enough to let either of them through. Well, gentlemen, what do you think they did? They just turned tail and scampered away as fast as they could in opposite directions. Now, England and America are like those bulldogs.

If modern leaders don't intuitively understand human nature as well as Lincoln did, they should at least make an attempt to learn more on the subject. After all, the most important asset a business organization has is its employees. So why not spend some time and money striving to more thoroughly understand what makes your people tick? All leaders, in every walk of life, should make this commitment to their followers. If they don't, they may soon find that they no longer qualify as leaders due to the simple fact that all their followers, in one way or another, have abandoned them.

Contemporary executives should also realize that successful alliances, whether with subordinates or other organizations, put the leader in a position of strength and power. And, conversely, divisiveness breeds weakness. Herein lies the wisdom of Lincoln's famous statement: "A house divided against itself cannot stand." That is one reason these words have lived on through the years, continually regarded as one of Lincoln's most important messages.

LINCOLN PRINCIPLES

- ★ Wage only one war at a time.
- ★ Spend time letting your followers learn that you are firm, resolute, and committed in the daily performance of your duty. Doing so will gain their respect and trust.
- ★ Etiquette and personal dignity are sometimes wisely set aside.
- ★ Invest time and money in better understanding the ins and outs of human nature.
- ★ Remember, human action can be modified to some extent, but human nature cannot be changed.
- ★ Showing your compassionate and caring nature will aid you in forging successful relationships.
- ★ When you extinguish hope, you create desperation.
- ★ You must remember that people who have not even been suspected of disloyalty are very adverse to taking an oath of any sort as a condition of exercising an ordinary right of citizenship.

> With public sentiment, nothing can fail; without it, nothing can succeed. Consequently he who molds public sentiment goes deeper than he who enacts statutes or pronounces decisions.

Lincoln's remarks in the first Lincoln–Douglas debate when examining the influence Stephen A. Douglas was having on the public (August 21, 1858)

3 / *Persuade Rather Than Coerce*

Abraham Lincoln strived to work with and through people while, at the same time, always driving to achieve his own main objective, which was preservation of the federal Union. He possessed an outgoing interest in people and had the ability to gain the confidence and respect of a wide variety of individuals. He was poised and confident under pressure, and he influenced others with his friendly manner, openness, and verbal skills.

Lincoln was not the dictator the unfriendly press of his day labeled him. Though he was decisive, especially in the expansion of executive authority, he almost always rejected coercion as a means of attaining what he desired. It's worthy to note that leadership, by definition, omits the use of coercive power. When a leader begins to coerce his followers, he's essentially abandoning leadership and embracing dictatorship. Lincoln rejected the dictatorial role by becoming a persuader-delegator in substance, style, and philosophy.

Looking into Lincoln's life as a state legislator, lawyer, and congressman, we can see that it was his mastery of the art of persuasion that brought him much of his success. In 1836, at the age of twenty-seven, during his second term in the Illinois legislature, Lincoln created the plan that moved the capital of the state from Vandalia to Springfield. His clever bargaining, coupled with persistence and personal persuasiveness, allowed him to pull off what was then regarded as a political coup. Later, as a lawyer, Lincoln not only had to convince juries and judges of his position, but his clients as well. In his notes for a law lecture, written in 1850, the forty-one-year-old future president advised his listeners: "Discourage litigation. *Persuade* your neighbors to compromise whenever you can." His remarks to the Springfield Washington Temperance Society in 1842 were perhaps his clearest enunciation of his philosophy regarding persuasion:

> When the conduct of men is designed to be influenced, *persuasion*, kind, unassuming persuasion, should ever be adopted. It is an old and a true maxim, that a "drop of honey catches more flies than a gallon of gall." So with men. If you would win a man to your cause, *first* convince him that you are his sincere friend. Therein is a drop of honey that catches his heart, which, say what he will, is the great high road to his reason, and which, when once gained, you will find but little trouble in convincing his judgment of the justice of your cause, if indeed that cause really be a just one. On the contrary, assume to dictate to his judgment, or to command his action, or to mark him as one to be shunned and despised, and he will retreat within himself, close all the avenues to his head and his heart; and tho' your cause be naked truth itself . . . you shall no more be able to

[reach] him, than to penetrate the hard shell of a tortoise with a rye straw.

Such is man, and so *must* he be understood by those who would *lead* him, even to his own best interest. [italics added]

Dictatorship, force, coercion—all were characteristics of tyrants, despots, and oppressors in Lincoln's view. All violated the basic rights of the individual to which he was so committed and upon which the nation was founded. All violated a basic sense of common decency. And here is where Lincoln tied in the Golden Rule and the law of the land to his personal leadership style. He treated people the way he would want to be treated, the way he knew others wanted to be treated.

Lincoln learned, refined, and mastered the art of persuasion during his early career. When he entered the political arena, he used his ability to persuade as a bridge to the voting public. He struck a chord with all people when he spoke out against slavery. No one wants to be forced to do something against his will. People generally want to believe that what they're doing truly makes a difference and, more important, that it is their own idea. Lincoln realized this fact, as should all potential leaders. During his rise to power, it was a heavy theme in his speeches and writings, somewhat camouflaged in his stance against slavery. And it was no small factor in his eventual success. "No man is good enough to govern another man without that other's consent," he remarked in 1854. "Familiarize yourselves with the chains of bondage," he said in 1858, "and you prepare your own limbs to wear them." And in 1859 he asserted: "Understanding the spirit of our institutions is to aim at the *elevation* of men; I am opposed to whatever tends to degrade them." Without question, dictatorship in any form degrades human beings.

Furthermore, in his day-to-day activities, Lincoln did not abandon his principles once he attained the White House. As president, Lincoln attempted to gain commitment from individuals through openness, empowerment, and coaching. He provided as much support, both moral and monetary, as he possibly could. He told his cabinet members that "in questions affecting the whole country there should be full and frequent consultations and that nothing should be done particularly affecting any department without consultation with the head of that department." And he especially supported his generals, even the procrastinating George McClellan, who was constantly criticized for his "deliberateness." For example, on the evening of October 26, 1861, three Senators called at the White House and demanded that Lincoln force McClellan into action. The president, however, defended his general and sent the legislators on their way. As soon as they were gone, he visited McClellan's home and, after a lengthy conference, assured the general that "we must not fight till you are ready." "I will hold McClellan's horse," Lincoln once said, "if he will only bring us success."

Unlike McClellan (with his "I can do it all" attitude), Lincoln was smart enough to know that *he* could not do it all. Each of his generals had to be his own man. If each was a leader in his own right, if each could take the responsibility, authority, and ownership of his assigned area of the war, then Lincoln would, in essence, have as many commanders-in-chief as he had generals. And *then* he would be able to mount a most formidable onslaught against the South, one that could not possibly be overcome.

Lincoln's problem, however, was that most of his generals were not willing to assume the responsibility of command, because they lacked either the courage or the ability. Consequently he was forced to take charge himself. Through most of his administration President Lincoln ran through a gauntlet of generals who could not do the job he demanded. These professional soldiers all had opportunities to take charge and win the war. Initially, they were given the same support that was accorded McClellan. Lincoln encouraged them to take initiative, to issue orders according to their own judgment, and to act without consulting him. In short, Lincoln exercised competent leadership—he delegated responsibility and authority, and empowered his subordinates to act on their own. All of them failed, however, causing Lincoln endless pain and anguish.

Lincoln could find only one general who would do what he wanted. On March 10, 1864, he appointed Ulysses S. Grant general-in-chief of the Army. Earlier in the war Grant had won impressive battles in Tennessee, had held tough and obtained a major victory at Vicksburg, and, as commander of the Department of the Mississippi and Department of the West, had proven his ability to fight and win. "Grant," Lincoln declared, "is the first general I have had. You know how it has been with all the rest. They wanted me to be the general. I am glad to find a man who can go ahead without me."

Was it worth it for Lincoln to wait for a man like Grant to come along? What *were* his options in the beginning, anyway? Could he have just taken over and run the entire military operation himself? Obviously, had he done so, Lincoln would have failed because he would not have been able to handle the other responsibilities of his executive position. It actually took Lincoln three full years to evolve the military system and its leadership into what it eventually became under U. S. Grant. Was it worth the wait? The amazing fact that he saved the nation alone justifies his action. Yet, Lincoln's long-term commitment to making things work (without deviating from his basic philosophy regarding persuasion, support, and delegation) paid off. By continuing his relentless search for a "real general," as Lincoln put it, he ended up doing the job sooner and more efficiently than he would have had he tried a more haphazard, less controlled, and desperate approach.

Holding the position of president of the United States gave Lincoln not only vast power but wide-ranging influence. He realized that to get things done his way, he did not have to issue an order but could merely imply something or make a suggestion. This was his chosen way, and it proved far more effective than commanding others to obey him. *Abraham Lincoln knew the value of making requests as opposed to issuing orders.* The letters and telegrams that he wrote to subordinates are filled with suggestions, views, and recommendations; rarely was there a direct order. He preferred to let his generals make their own decisions and hoped that, through his suggestions, they would do the right thing. Here are some examples:

> To MCCLELLAN (*10-13-63*): ". . . This letter is in no sense an order."
>
> To HALLECK (*9-19-63*): "I hope you will consider it . . ."
>
> To BURNSIDE (*9-27-63*): "It was suggested to you, not ordered. . . ."
>
> To BANKS (*1-13-64*): "Frame orders, and fix times and places, for this, and that, according to your own judgment."
>
> To GRANT (*4-30-64*): "If there is anything wanting which is within my power to give, do not fail to let me know it."

Relating a well-chosen story or anecdote was his chief form of persuasion in getting others to come around to his side. Lincoln once attempted to convince his secretary of the treasury, Salmon P. Chase, that it was a good idea for the government to issue interest-bearing currency as a means of raising money to support the war effort. Chase, however, objected to the proposal and argued that it was unconstitutional. Rather than simply ordering Chase to do it, which he could have as president, Lincoln chose to tell him the story of an Italian captain who ran his vessel on a rock and knocked a hole in her bottom. He set his men to pumping, and he went to pray before a figure of the Virgin in the bow of the ship. The leak gained on them. It looked at last as if the vessel would go down with all on board. The captain, at length, in a fit of rage at not having his prayers answered, seized the figure of the Virgin and threw it overboard. Suddenly the leak stopped, the water was pumped out, and the vessel got safely to port. When docked for repairs the statue of the Virgin Mary was found stuck, head foremost, in the hole.

Chase at first didn't see the precise application of the story. "Why, Chase," responded Lincoln, "I don't intend precisely to throw the Virgin Mary overboard, and by that I mean the Constitution, but I will stick it in the hole if I can. These rebels are violating the Constitution in order to destroy the Union; I will violate the Constitution, if necessary, to save the Union; and I suspect, Chase, that our Constitution is going to have a rough time of it before we get done with this row."

Another method of persuasion Lincoln often used was to write long, detailed letters to his subordinates. Perhaps the best single source illustrating Lincoln's attitude and philosophy regarding persuasion, support, and delegation lies in his remarkable letter to Gen. Joseph Hooker, written on the occasion of the general's appointment to command the Army of the Potomac. The president had dismissed Gen. Ambrose Burnside (after Burnside demanded the removal of Hooker as a corps commander) and then named Hooker in his place. Lincoln had been frustrated with Burnside's inaction and was looking for someone to lead the army into battle. Hooker was widely known by his nickname, "Fighting Joe," and that seemed good enough for the president. The appointment was also consistent with Lincoln's tendency to select men whom he felt would be action-oriented. However, there were also some problems regarding the general's conduct that Lincoln felt he had to address. Hooker constantly criticized and argued with his superiors. In addition, after the battle of Fredericksburg, he had suggested that what the country needed was a dictator.

Now here is where Lincoln was confronted with a unique problem. What were his options? He could simply have ignored Hooker and not appointed him at all. In fact, Lincoln had every reason *not* to appoint this arrogant general. But he was desperate to find a general who would take the initiative and he believed, at the time, that "Fighting Joe" would do just that. So Lincoln decided to take a chance on Hooker, but he used the same style of persuasion, support, and encouragement that he had used with all the previous generals.

On January 26, 1863, Lincoln summoned his new commander to Washington, where the two discussed Hooker's attitudes along with sweeping strategies for pursuing the war effort. Through the course of their conversation, Lincoln told Hooker what he expected and, at the end of the meeting, so that the general could ponder the issues more thoroughly, Lincoln handed him this now famous letter:

EXECUTIVE MANSION

Washington

January 26, 1863

Major General Hooker:

General.

I have placed you at the head of the Army of the Potomac. Of course, I have done this upon what appears to me to be sufficient reasons. And yet I think it best for you to know that there are some things in regard to which, I am not quite satisfied with you. I believe you to be a brave and skillful soldier, which, of course, I like. I also believe you do not mix politics with your profession, in which you are right. You have confidence in yourself, which is a valuable, if not an indispensable quality. You are ambitious, which, within reasonable bounds, does good rather than harm. But I think that during Gen. Burnside's command of the

Army, you have taken counsel of your ambition, and thwarted him as much as you could, in which you did a great wrong to the country, and to a most meritorious and honorable brother officer. I have heard, in such a way as to believe it, of your recently saying that both the Army and the Government needed a Dictator. Of course it was not *for* this, but in spite of it, that I have given you the command. Only those generals who gain successes, can set up dictators. What I now ask of you is military success, and I will risk the dictatorship. The government will support you to the utmost of its ability, which is neither more nor less than it has done and will do for all commanders. I much fear that the spirit which you have aided to infuse into the Army, of criticizing their Commander, and withholding confidence from him, will now turn upon you. I shall assist you as far as I can, to put it down. Neither you, nor Napoleon, if he were alive again, could get any good out of an army, while such a spirit prevails in it.

And now, beware of rashness. Beware of rashness, but with energy, and sleepless vigilance, go forward, and give us victories.

Yours very truly
A. Lincoln

Contemporary leaders can learn an important lesson from this letter. For here, in one bold stroke, Lincoln told Hooker exactly what he thought of him (both good and bad) and precisely what he expected; he offered support and assistance; and he encouraged his general to take the initiative and do the right thing. Then Lincoln handed Hooker the letter so that he could take it with him and ponder their conversation more thoroughly. Here was Lincoln the leader at his best.

And General Hooker was deeply impressed. Several months

later, he remarked to a newspaperman that this communiqué was "just such a letter as a father might write to his son."

Leadership often involves parenting, and Lincoln's fatherly tendencies aided him in his position as president. The organization is the family; the leader is the head of the family. Consequently, leaders often nurture and guide subordinates much as parents do children.

It's not called the "art of persuasion" for nothing. This intangible, often elusive, skill was a mainstay in Lincoln's interaction arsenal. He was adept at stepping in when subordinates had just missed gaining victory. He constantly modeled the tenets that he preached. He rendered discipline in a fatherly way. All of this formed the basis for a consistent, reliable method to persuade *and* produce.

With today's employees wanting more than monetary and tangible rewards, leaders need to use different persuasive tactics than the traditional "stick and carrot" approach. Understanding the nuances of various positions and building rapport with a variety of workers allows you to take the most effective path to success without damaging relationships.

LINCOLN PRINCIPLES

★ Discourage formal grievances. *Persuade* your subordinates to compromise whenever you can.

★ Use force only as a last resort.

★ Remember that your followers generally want to believe that what they do is their own idea and, more importantly, that it genuinely makes a difference.

★ If you would win a subordinate to your cause, *first* convince him that you are his sincere friend.

★ Seek the consent of your followers for you to lead them.

★ If you practice dictatorial leadership, you prepare yourself to be dictated to.

★ Delegate responsibility and authority by empowering people to act on their own.

★ On issues that affect your entire organization, conduct full and frequent consultations with the heads of your various departments.

★ A good leader avoids issuing orders, preferring to request, imply, or make suggestions.

PART II
CHARACTER

I am compelled to take a more impartial and unprejudiced view of things. Without claiming to be your superior, which I do not, my position enables me to understand my duty in all these matters better than you possibly can, and I hope you do not yet doubt my integrity.

Lincoln's closing comments in a letter of support for General-in-Chief Henry Halleck to a close friend who urged his dismissal (May 26, 1863)

4 / *Honesty and Integrity Are the Best Policies*

Part of the Lincoln myth is that Abraham Lincoln was fair, trustworthy, sincere, straightforward, of sound moral principle and, like George Washington, truthful. He even had the nickname "Honest Abe." During the 1830s, Lincoln formed a partnership with William Berry to open and run a general store in New Salem, Illinois. It was probably in this period that he picked up his nickname, having become known as a fair and honest businessman. He was also quite popular in the small town, where everyone seemed to know him well, especially after he secured the position of postmaster. Popularity and honesty, however, don't always make a business run, and Lincoln and his partner "did nothing but get deeper and deeper in debt," and, as Lincoln later phrased it, "the store winked out." Part of the reason for the failure was that Berry was a heavy drinker, and, when he died in 1835, Lincoln was left with the responsibility of repaying the large sum of $1,100

(Lincoln termed it "the national debt"). It took him many years, but pay it back he did, every penny.

The moniker "Honest Abe" was resurrected for the presidential campaign in 1860. A major component of the Republican campaign hype, it was plastered on campaign posters and appeared in cartoons and newspapers across the country. It was all part of a national crusade that painted Lincoln as one of the common people, a railsplitter from Illinois who was honest beyond question. It has remained in the American stream of consciousness to this day, as perhaps the most glorified part of the Lincoln myth.

But as American philosopher William Ernest Hocking noted: "there are myths which displace truth and there are myths which give wings to truth." In this case, Abraham Lincoln's reputation for honesty and integrity, even though challenged over the years, has remained unblemished. In fact, as knowledge is gained about the real man, it is largely enhanced. Myth in this case has become reality. Lincoln was just as honest as he has been purported to be, if not more so. Without question honesty is one of the major qualities that made him a great leader.

The architecture of leadership, all the theories and guidelines, falls apart without honesty and integrity. It's the keystone that holds an organization together. Tom Peters reported in his research that the best, most aggressive, and successful organizations were the ones that stressed integrity and trust. "Without doubt," Peters stated, "honesty has always been the best policy." "Managers do things right. Leaders do the right thing," wrote Bennis and Nanus. James MacGregor Burns warned: "Divorced from ethics, leadership is reduced to management and politics to mere technique."

Integrity must be sincere. That's one reason Lincoln was so admired in his lifetime. Through an individual's words, deeds, and actions, integrity can be judged to be genuine. And integrity is tied closely to the values espoused by an effective leader. As a rule, leaders must set and respond to fundamental goals and values that move their followers. In addition to being much-needed moral standards, values tend to be motives by which subordinates act and react. The possession and preaching of wide-ranging, appealing goals and values will result in broad support from the masses. People will be involved participants in a shared group effort. Put more simply, values motivate.

Any successful organization, whether a business or a country, must possess strong shared values. These values must be "owned" by not only the vast majority of the organization, but in some cases by all its members. But how in the world can every member of any group share, and be committed to, the same set of values? This is where the leader comes in. It is the sole responsibility of the leader to instill these values by constant preaching and persuasion. It is the leader's role to lift followers out of their everyday selves up to a higher level of awareness, motivation, and commitment.

Lincoln constantly shared, stressed, and reemphasized the two most fundamental values that, over the years, have mobilized Americans: "the pursuit of liberty" and "equality." His integrity was, in short, the nation's integrity. "I have never had a feeling politically that did not spring from the sentiments embodied in the Declaration of Independence," he once said. All men were created equal in Lincoln's eyes, and the nation was formed by the founding fathers so that any tyrant who might "reappear in this fair land and commence their vocation, . . . should find left for them at least one hard nut to crack."

For Lincoln the Civil War was not just a conflict in arms but, rather, a "people's contest." "On the side of the Union," he said, it was "a struggle for maintaining in the world that form and substance of government whose leading object is to elevate the condition of men . . . to afford all an unfettered start, and a fair chance, in the race of life."

With such inspiring words, it is no wonder that Abraham Lincoln was able to motivate and mobilize the Union government and its citizens so effectively. He appealed to everyone's basic sense of decency and integrity.

But Lincoln also practiced what he preached. When he made it to the top he would turn and reach down for the person behind him, helping to "elevate" that person to his better self. He would help others climb the ladder of success with patience, trust, and respect. In so doing, Lincoln was what Burns termed a "sharing leader"; one of those leaders who "perceive their roles as shaping the future to the advantage of groups with which they identify, and advantage they define in terms of the broadest possible goals and the highest possible levels of morality."

Trust, honesty, and integrity are exceedingly important qualities because they so strongly affect followers. Most individuals need to trust others, especially their boss. Subordinates must perceive their leader as a consistently fair person if they're to engage in the kind of innovative risk-taking that brings a company rewards.

Lincoln always did the right thing, or at least he attempted to do so. He simply did not deal with people he knew to be dishonest. "Stand with anybody that stands right," he preached. "Stand with him while he is right and part with him when he goes wrong." Lincoln basically fired Simon Cameron, his first secretary of war, for improprieties in awarding defense contracts and other shady dealings. He authorized no bargains at the 1860 Republican Convention (even though many were made without his knowledge). And he advised others to "never add the weight of your character to a charge against a person without *knowing* it to be true." Now isn't this the type of person you would like to be associated with and do business with? Isn't it obvious that Lincoln could be trusted, that he had integrity?

Lincoln would also become disdainful and enraged whenever dishonesty, in whatever form, reared its head. Many of his stories, anecdotes, and colloquial expressions were aimed at liars, swindlers, and cheats. He could compare an individual who smiles and then stabs you in the back to a tree that was being killed by a vine that covered its trunk: "It's like certain habits of men," said Lincoln. "It decorates the ruin it makes." And he would mock those who would do wrong and then accuse others by comparing them to the ruffian who made an unprovoked assault in the street upon a quiet citizen: "The criminal drew his revolver, but the assaulted party made a sudden spring and wrested the weapon from the hands of the would-be assassin. 'Stop!' said the attacker. 'Give me back that pistol; you have no right to my property.'"

At one point during the war, Lincoln was forced by his cabinet to confront the realization that many people who were thought to be Union patriots were actually spies providing key information to the Confederacy. Not only was the situation a security concern, but Lincoln was particularly distressed at the obvious lack of loyalty and honesty from so many people who were believed to be Union supporters. After presenting all the evidence, Secretary of War Stanton turned to the president and asked for direction. Lincoln, who had been silent and visibly disturbed, expressed his feelings with a story about the dilemma of an old farmer who had a very large shade tree towering over his house:

> It was a majestic-looking tree, and apparently perfect in every part—tall, straight, and of immense size—the grand old sentinel of his forest home. One morning, while at work in his garden, he saw a squirrel [run up the tree into a hole] and thought the tree might be hollow. He proceeded to examine it carefully and, much to his surprise, he found that the stately [tree] that he had [valued] for its beauty and grandeur to be the pride and protection of his little farm was hollow from top to bottom. Only a rim of sound wood remained, barely sufficient to support its weight. What was he to do? If he cut it down, it would [do great damage] with its great length and spreading branches.

If he let it remain, his family was in constant danger. In a storm it might fall, or the wind might blow it down, and his house and children be crushed by it. What should he do? As he turned away, he said sadly: "I wish I had never seen that squirrel."

By today's standards, the moniker "Honest Abe" might be considered pretentious, even contrived. But the fact is that leaders who tell their subordinates the truth, even when the news is bad, gain greater respect and support for ideas than their less virtuous counterparts.

Even though he had some detractors, Lincoln attained success, admiration, and a positive image by maintaining his integrity and honesty. Those who questioned his upbringing and education, or even his political affiliations, tended not to doubt his integrity.

Lincoln showed the same degree of fairness and decency whether disciplining or congratulating a subordinate. Emulating his style will earn leaders the trust and respect that ultimately foster passionate commitment. This approach shows that the truth is a common denominator for all interactions, among any group, and with people of varying personalities.

LINCOLN PRINCIPLES

★ Give your subordinates a fair chance with equal freedom and opportunity for success.

★ When you make it to the top, turn and reach down for the person behind you.

★ You must set, and respond to, fundamental goals and values that move your followers.

★ You must be consistently fair and decent, in both the business and the personal side of life.

★ Stand with anybody who stands right. Stand with him while he is right and part with him when he goes wrong.

★ Never add the weight of your character to a charge against a person without *knowing* it to be true.

★ It is your duty to advance the aims of the organization and also to help those who serve it.

★ If you once forfeit the confidence of your fellow citizens, you can never regain their respect and esteem.

I shall do nothing in malice. What I deal with is too vast for malicious dealing.

Lincoln's comments in a letter about the readmission of Louisiana to the Union (July 28, 1862)

5 / Never Act Out of Vengeance or Spite

Followers in virtually every organization respond better to, and will more easily be led by, a leader who consistently displays kindness and empathy than one who is associated with vindictiveness or animosity. This, of course, is only human nature, and Abraham Lincoln seemed to instinctively realize it. Moreover, he understood that to actively engage in slander and malicious dealings would simply eat up far too much of his time, which he used in securing positive end results rather than negative ones. Pettiness, spite, and vengeance are emotional reactions considered to be beneath the dignity of a leader. Followers expect their leaders to rise above such demeaning and degrading activity.

While kindness was the very foundation of his personality, Lincoln also understood that if people were going to come to him with ideas, suggestions, and better ways of making things work, he had to provide the climate to allow it. He actively encouraged innovative thinking and the participation of sub-ordinates. Lincoln wanted to "adopt new views so fast as they shall appear to be true views."

And it was those "true views"—*the truth*—that guided Lincoln through his stormy, turbulent tenure in office. Whenever he had doubts, and there must have been many, he fell back on the foundation of his personality: honesty, integrity, compassion, and mercy. He seemed to have virtually no feelings of hate, vindictiveness, or malice. Many people of his day, in fact, thought his tendency toward leniency was over-done. He granted more pardons, for example, than any president had before him—or has since.

Lincoln kept warrants for execution, marked "cowardice in the face of the enemy," pigeonholed in the desk in his office and referred to them as his "leg cases," "running itch," or "vulnerable heels." "I put it to you," he once remarked, "and I leave it for you to decide for yourself. If Almighty God gives a man a cowardly pair of legs, how can he help their running away with him?" With this philosophy in hand, Lincoln would scrawl on the back of an envelope containing a request for clemency a simple "Let it be done." In one case he saved a sixteen-year-old-boy from the firing squad by telegraphing Gen. George Meade that he was "unwilling for any boy under eighteen to be shot."

Even the president's two sons, Willie and Tad, were aware of their father's frequent pardons. Having sentenced their doll soldier to death as punishment for sleeping on guard duty, they obtained mercy from their father. "The doll Jack is pardoned. By order of the President," he commanded on Executive Mansion stationery, signing it just as he signed all of his pardons: A. Lincoln.

President Lincoln felt that the wanton execution of desert-ing soldiers was not only improper but that it also damaged the nation. In a statement that sounds as though it came from someone who was both a savvy businessman and an honest lawyer, Lincoln once wrote: "When neither incompetency, nor intentional wrong, nor real injury to the service is imputed—

in such cases it is both cruel and impolitic, to crush the man and make him and his friends permanent enemies to the administration, if not to the government itself." "The government," he later commented, "has a difficult duty to perform. At the very best, it will by turns do both too little and too much. It can properly have no motive of revenge, no purpose to punish merely for punishment's sake. While we must, by all available means, prevent the overthrow of the government, we should avoid planting and cultivating too many thorns in the bosom of society."

What can modern leaders infer from Lincoln's issuance of so many pardons? Is there a lesson to be learned here? It is, in part, that by being compassionate and kind rather than malicious or vengeful, a leader will make fewer enemies for himself and his organization and will thereby create more supporters, more dedicated "soldiers" to aid in the overall corporate mission. For each man Lincoln pardoned, he returned a loyal veteran to the military to carry on the struggle for preservation of the Union.

By the later stages of the Civil War, knowledge of Lincoln's compassion, his ability to forgive, and his general unwillingness to take harsh actions had spread throughout the nation, even to the Southern states. In February 1865, he left Washington to conduct the Hampton Roads Peace Conference, where he met with several Confederate leaders. During that meeting, the conversation eventually got around to their fate. Lincoln stated unequivocally that they had forfeited all right to immunity from punishment. After a long pause, one of the Southerners addressed the president: "Then, Mr. President, if we understand you correctly, you think that we of the Confederacy have committed treason; that we are traitors to your government; that we have forfeited our rights, and are proper subjects for the hangman. Is that not about what your words imply?"

"Yes, you have stated the proposition better than I did," said Lincoln. "That is about the size of it."

"Well, Mr. Lincoln," the commissioner replied after another pause, "we have about concluded that we shall not be hanged as long as you are President—if we behave ourselves."

Did knowing about Lincoln's compassionate nature give the Confederate leaders courage to seek the opportunity to gain an audience with Lincoln? Did it make him more approachable? Obviously, if people, whether business associates or subordinates, realize that a leader is not given to spite and pettiness, they will be more willing to openly seek him out. This will, in turn, make the leader more effective.

Not only would he not execute Confederate officials; if Lincoln had his way he would let them all go free. "Frighten them out of the country," he urged, "open the gates, let down the bars, scare them off!" Gen. William Tecumseh Sherman, who already knew that it was "very hard for the President to hang spies," once asked Lincoln explicitly whether he wanted Jefferson Davis captured or allowed to escape. Lincoln replied:

> I'll tell you, General, what I think of taking Jeff Davis. Out in Illinois there was an old temperance lecturer who was very strict in the doctrine and practice of total abstinence. One day, after a long ride in the hot sun, he stopped at the house of a friend, who proposed making him a lemonade. When the friend asked if he wouldn't like a drop of something stronger in the drink, he replied that he couldn't think of it. "I'm opposed to it on principle," he said. "But," he added with a longing glance at the bottle that stood conveniently at hand, "if you could manage to put in a drop unbeknownst to me, I guess it wouldn't hurt me much." Now, General, I am bound to oppose the escape of Jeff Davis; but if you could manage to let him slip out *unbeknownst-like*, I guess it wouldn't hurt me much.

"And that," General Sherman later remarked, "is all I could get out of the Government as to what its policy was concerning the rebel leaders until Stanton assailed me for Davis' escape."

When the curtain finally came down on the South at the end of the Civil War, it was Lincoln who, in a dramatic gesture of goodwill, requested the playing of "Dixie" at a rally outside the White House: "I have always thought 'Dixie' one of the best tunes I have ever heard," he said. "Our adversaries over the way attempted to appropriate it, but I insisted yesterday that we fairly captured it. I presented the question to the Attorney General, and he gave it as his legal opinion that it is our lawful prize. I now request the band to favor me with its performance." This strong statement let others know that Lincoln would not seek revenge now that the war had ended. It was a policy that he'd brought to Washington when he became president, and he wouldn't abandon it now that he had achieved his goal.

Such a gesture not only impressed the people of the Confederacy; it also let Lincoln's followers know that there would be no vengeance sought against the South as long as he was in charge. Invariably an organization takes on the personality of its top leader, providing that individual is in touch with the members of the organization. If the leader is petty, the subordinates will be petty. But if the leader is encouraging, optimistic, and courteous, then the vast majority of the workers in the organization will be as well.

Abraham Lincoln was not a vengeful person. "What I deal with is too vast for malicious dealing," he said. Rather, he welcomed the South back with open arms and, in his Second Inaugural Address, he asked his fellow countrymen to do the same. In the closing remarks of the address, which has been called his "Sermon on the Mount," Lincoln revealed in most eloquent terms the depth of his conviction:

> With malice toward none; with charity for all; with firmness in the right as God gives us to see the right, let us strive on to finish the work we are in, to bind up the

nation's wounds, to care for him who shall have borne
the battle and for his widow and his orphan, to do all
which may achieve and cherish a just and lasting peace
among ourselves, and with all nations.

With remarks like this, it was obvious that Lincoln was going
to treat the defeated Confederates the same way he treated the
men he whipped wrestling in his youth: he would "let 'em up
easy."

In general, a lack of malice on the part of a leader—genuine
caring—inspires trust among subordinates and fosters innovative thinking. It also keeps followers from being terrified,
allowing them to be themselves. Contemporary leaders should
adopt Lincoln's style and "pardon" mistakes as opposed to
chewing out subordinates.

LINCOLN PRINCIPLES

★ Never crush a man out, thereby making him and his friends permanent enemies of your organization.

★ No purpose is served by punishing merely for punishment's sake.

★ Always keep in mind that once a subordinate is destroyed he ceases to contribute to the organization.

★ People will be more willing to seek an audience with you if you have a good reputation.

★ It would not hurt you much if, once in a while, you could manage to let things slip, *unbeknownst-like.*

★ Remember: Your organization will take on the personality of its top leader.

★ You should be very unwilling for young people to be ruined for slight causes.

★ Have malice toward none and charity for all.

★ Touch people with the better angels of your nature.

Neither let us be slandered from our duty by false accusations against us, nor frightened from it by menaces of destruction to the government, nor of dungeons to ourselves. Let us have faith that right makes might, and in that faith let us to the end dare to do our duty as we understand it.

> The closing statement of Lincoln's Cooper Institute Address, in which he encouraged party members to hold fast to their beliefs (February 27, 1860)

6 / *Have the Courage to Handle Unjust Criticism*

Grace under pressure" was Ernest Hemingway's definition of courage. And three words were never more appropriate to describe the demeanor of Abraham Lincoln during the last seven years of his life.

Without question, Lincoln displayed an amazing amount of courage over an extended period of time. He survived numerous setbacks and defeats (such as the Illinois senate election of 1858 and early Civil War battles), only to overcome them all and persistently endure until obtaining the final victory. Through it all, Lincoln was the risk-taker, assuming a bold stand and not wavering in the process. He had faith and confidence in himself and didn't need ego-stroking or constant reinforcement to know that this course of action was proper.

Armed rebellion against the Union provided an extraordinary showcase for Lincoln's talents. The ability to understand the reality of the situation and then confront it decisively made him a most formidable leader. Moreover, he was able to formulate a strategy and then communicate both the strategy and the reality of civil war, whether or not people wanted to hear them.

"Telling it like it was" brought forth enormous amounts of censure upon Lincoln from all directions. But every man of courage must, sooner or later, deal with unjust criticism. And all individuals who lead other people, especially those who enter the political arena, likely will be subjected to severe criticism as well as personal attacks on their honor and character. Lincoln realized this fact of life and was prepared for it, as every leader should be.

Abraham Lincoln was slandered, libeled, and hated perhaps more intensely than any man ever to run for the nation's highest office. He won the election of 1860 largely because the Democratic party was hopelessly split, having fielded two candidates—Stephen A. Douglas from the North and John C. Breckenridge from the South. Lincoln was the first president elected from the Republican party, which was well unified with a strong support base in the Northeast. Lincoln's name, in fact, was not even on the ballot in most Southern states. As a result of his election (by a minority of votes cast), the South seceded, the Civil War began, and criticism of Lincoln reached maximum proportions. Most of the nation could not comprehend how this seemingly awkward country lawyer from the West had been elected president.

He was publicly called just about every name imaginable by the press of the day, including a grotesque baboon, a third-rate country lawyer who once split rails and now splits the Union, a coarse vulgar joker, a dictator, an ape, a buffoon, and others. The *Illinois State Register* labeled him "the craftiest and most dishonest politician that ever disgraced an office in America." One can only imagine what it must have been like and what was going through Lincoln's mind when he reached Washington to take the oath of office. He gave an indication that he was ever mindful of these feelings toward him when, shortly before his inauguration, he related to a group of people: "I have reached this city of Washington under circumstances considerably differing from those under which any other man has ever reached it. I have reached it for the purpose of taking an official position amongst the people, almost all of whom were opposed to me, and are yet opposed to me, as I suppose."

Severe and unjust criticism did not subside after Lincoln took the oath of office, nor did it come only from Southern sympathizers. It came from within the Union itself, from Congress, from some factions within the Republican party, and, initially, from within his own cabinet. As president, Lincoln learned that, no matter what he did, there were going to be people who would not be pleased. In his first year, he was required to fill many vacant government positions by appointment. Regarding each vacancy, he once remarked: ". . . there are twenty applicants, and of these I must make nineteen enemies." As his enemies increased, so did the criticism against him. But Lincoln handled it all with a patience, forbearance, and determination uncommon of most men. He was philosophical about it all and, in part, fell back on his understanding of people. "Human nature will not change," he said in 1864. "In any future great national trial, compared with the men of this, we shall have as weak and as strong, as silly and as wise, as bad and as good."

Throughout much of his life, Lincoln was the object of jealousy, envy, and malice. This was largely the result of his burning desire for achievement, which motivated him to excel. People whom he surpassed in his advancement naturally vented their jealous emotions against him through verbal attacks. As a young man, Lincoln must have felt great pain from these attackers. Time and maturity aided him in dealing with such criticism later in life, but he never forgot the feelings he'd experienced. As a result, he had great compassion for others who were subjected to the same treatment. A young doctor once related how Lincoln had successfully defended him in a malpractice suit, thereby saving his career:

> When I asked for my bill, [Lincoln] said: "You are a young man just starting out upon your career. I have earned a hundred dollars. I am only going to charge you twenty-five, and I will donate the other seventy-five to a worthy young man who has been the subject of envy and malice."

In his four years as president, Lincoln endured all of the cruel antagonism and severe criticism directed at him. And the fact is, that he not only endured the slander but overcame it to secure victory in the Civil War and preserve the nation—a most amazing achievement. In the process, he also reorganized the American military system, expanded the limits of presidential authority, abolished slavery, and renewed the spirit of patriotism in America.

Modern leaders might find it interesting and helpful to explore Lincoln's methods in hearing, dealing with, and overcoming severe and unjust criticism. Lincoln handled such defamation in several different ways. Most often, he would simply ignore the attacks. This was particularly true of those times in the midst of political campaigns when most of the slander was petty and utterly ridiculous in nature. He had no time for it. He was too busy trying to win a war. Even though he would become very weary and discouraged by all the attacks upon him, when it came right down to it, he normally would not retaliate against his detractors. In the later part of 1864, at a time close to an election in which he could be voted out of office, the president kept his faith in the people. Lincoln believed that, in the end, his course would be vindicated. "I cannot run the political machine," he once said, "I have enough on my hands without that. It is the people's business—the election is in their hands. If they turn their backs to the fire, and get scorched in the rear, they'll find they have to sit on the blister."

Although he avoided reading anything that was an overt attack against him, Lincoln could not help but hear much of the criticism. During his early political years, he was consistently annoyed and hurt most by criticism that came from people he believed to be his friends. But, with time, Lincoln became toughened to the world of the political misrepresentation. He had the courage to carry with him to the White House his main strategy of simply ignoring slander and vilification. During his last public address, delivered April 11, 1865, he summed up years of experience in dealing with malicious criticism when he said: "As a general rule, I abstain from reading the reports of attacks upon myself, wishing not to be provoked by that to which I can not properly offer an answer."

However, on occasion Lincoln would stand up and defend himself to any and all detractors, especially if the false accusation was particularly damaging to the public's view of his principles. And when those principles were contrary to the beliefs of the local majority, Lincoln would not back down or compromise. In 1858, he may have lost the Illinois state senate race largely for his stance on slavery. Before one of the Lincoln–Douglas debates, Stephen A. Douglas was applauded and cheered loudly while Lincoln was virtually ignored. When some of his friends expressed concern over the cold reception, Lincoln passed over it lightly and courageously replied: "I am not going to be terrified by an excited populace, and hindered from speaking my honest sentiments upon this infernal subject of human slavery."

Michael Dukakis, who may have lost his bid for the presidency in 1988 because he did not strike back against Republican party criticism, might have acted differently had he remembered what Abraham Lincoln said during a speech in 1859. Reflecting upon his defeat at the hands of Douglas the prior year, Lincoln remarked: "I have found that it is not entirely safe, when one is misrepresented under his very nose, to allow the misrepresentation to go uncontradicted."

In 1864, while giving a speech at Baltimore, Lincoln defended his position against slavery, asserting: "The shepherd drives the wolf from the sheep's throat, for which the sheep thanks the shepherd as a *liberator*, while the wolf denounces him for the same act as the destroyer of liberty, especially as the sheep is a black one."

One of Lincoln's most effective methods of dealing with harsh criticism was to write extended letters of refutation. Often, in order to vent his anger and frustration, he would sit down at his desk, compose a letter of denial, and then walk away without sending it. He felt better for having stated his case but did not want any of his angry or emotional remarks made public.

Late in the election year 1864, Lincoln drafted a statement of refutation regarding a misrepresentation of the facts in what was popularly called "the Antietam episode." In October 1862, he'd visited the battlefield of Antietam and, while riding in a carriage on his way to review the Union troops, Lincoln asked his old friend Ward Lamon to sing one of his favorite melancholy songs. Lamon did sing a short, sad song and then, in an effort to raise the president's spirits, followed with several lighthearted tunes. A few months later it was reported in newspapers that President Lincoln had requested a happy song in the middle of the carnage of Antietam. The incident was resurrected again for the 1864 presidential election, when the *New York World* printed the following story:

ONE OF MR. LINCOLN'S JOKES—The second verse of our campaign song published on this page was probably suggested by an incident which occurred on the battle-field of Antietam a few days after the fight. While the President was driving over the field in an ambulance, accompanied by Marshal Lamon, General McClellan, and another officer, heavy details of men were engaged in the task of burying the dead. The ambulance had just reached the neighborhood of the old stone bridge, where the dead were piled highest, when Mr. Lincoln, suddenly slapping Marshal Lamon on the knee, exclaimed: "Come, Lamon, give us that song about Picayune Butler; McClellan has never heard it." "Not now, if you please," said General McClellan, with a shudder; "I would prefer to hear it some other place and time."

Lamon, outraged at the brutal attack on the president, suggested that he publicly deny the charges. At first Lincoln refused, saying: "There has already been too much said about this falsehood. Let the thing alone. If I have not established a character enough to give the lie to this charge, I can only say that I am mistaken in my own estimate of myself. In politics, every man must skin his own skunk. These fellows are welcome to the hide of this one. Its body has already given forth its unsavory odor."

Several days later, however, Ward Lamon drafted a reply of his own and presented it for approval to the president, who responded as follows:

No, Lamon, I would not publish this reply; it is too belligerent in tone for so grave a matter. There is a heap of "cussedness" mixed up with your usual amiability, and you are at times too fond of a fight. If I were you, I would simply state the facts as they were. I would give the statements as you have here, without the pepper and salt. Let me try my hand at it.

President Lincoln then proceeded to write a rather lengthy letter explaining the truth about the incident, including the facts that he visited Antietam sixteen days after the battle and that no dead bodies were seen. The letter was originally intended to be sent out as having been authored by Lamon, but Lincoln would not allow the response to be published. It was, in fact, not revealed to the general public until 1895.

Lincoln attempted to avoid provocation whenever possible by looking at the humorous side of any potentially hazardous situation. He was aided, as always, by his keen sense of humor, his sharp wit, and his arsenal of stories and anecdotes. It is a tribute to Lincoln that he could view unjust slander and criticism with amusement rather than anger. In 1858, when Stephen A. Douglas made several false charges against him, Lincoln began a reply by stating: "When a man hears himself somewhat misrepresented, it provokes him—at least, I find it so with myself; but when the misrepresentation becomes very gross and palpable, it is more apt to amuse him."

Lincoln carried his sense of humor straight into the White House, and it never failed him when he used it to ease the sting of a political slur. Often, by telling an appropriate story, he could effectively turn the tables on an antagonist. In one instance, Lincoln shot down a particularly offensive speaker by stating that "the oratory of the gentleman completely suspends all action of his mind." He compared the speaker to a steamboat, saying:

> Back in the days when I performed my part as a keel boatman, I made the acquaintance of a trifling little steamboat which used to bustle and puff and wheeze about in the Sangamon River. It had a five-foot boiler and a seven-foot whistle, and every time it whistled the boat stopped.

On another occasion, Lincoln was assailed by a Northern governor about his draft policy, insinuating that he would not carry out the president's orders. Lincoln, however, would not back down and ordered Secretary of War Stanton to go right ahead with the draft:

> The governor is like the boy I saw once at the launching of a ship. When everything was ready, they picked out a boy and sent him under the ship to knock away the trigger and let her go. At the critical moment everything depended on the boy. He had to do the job well

by a direct, vigorous blow, and then lie flat and keep
still while the ship slid over him. The boy did everything right; but he yelled as if he were being murdered,
from the time he got under the keel until he got out. I
thought the skin was all scraped off his back; but he
wasn't hurt at all. The master of the yard told me that
this boy was always chosen for that job, that he did his
work well, that he never had been hurt, but that he
always squealed in that way. That's just the way with
the governor. Make up your minds that he is not hurt,
and that he is doing his work right, and pay no
attention to his squealing. He only wants to make you
understand how hard his task is, and that he is on hand
performing it.

In addition to humor, Lincoln's strength was enhanced by
his ability to perceive reality and deal with it accordingly. He
once remarked to a group of people that "the pioneers in any
movement are not generally the best people to carry that
movement to a successful issue. They often have to meet such
hard opposition, and get so battered and bespattered, that
afterward, when people find they have to accept reform, they
will accept it more easily from others." And he knew going in
that "the Presidency, even to the most experienced politicians,
is no bed of roses. . . . No human being," he said, "can fill
that station and escape censure."

An overwhelming confidence in his own ability to know
right from wrong also gave Lincoln great strength to combat
unjust criticism. He was not intimidated when so many others
took a position that he considered to be morally unjust.
Neither would he back down in the face of harsh accusations
against his own beliefs. "It often requires more courage to dare
to do right than to fear to do wrong," he once said. "He who
has the right needs not to fear," he wrote to Gen. John
McClernand. ". . . *truth* is generally the best vindication
against slander," he told Horace Greeley.

Contemporary leaders, especially those in the political arena, can take heart and gain great strength from knowing that Lincoln succeeded, and from understanding his methods in overcoming adversity. You must have stamina, fortitude, and self-confidence. You must believe in yourself. But, in addition, a certain style and routine must be developed in dealing with harsh criticism. Every leader will encounter such slander simply by virtue of the position held. It is how you let it affect you that makes the difference in whether or not you succeed.

Do what Lincoln did. Ignore most of the attacks if they are petty, but fight back when they are important enough to make a difference. Write letters of refutation that vent your anger and emotions, but do not mail them. And, always, look at the lighter side of life by keeping your sense of humor.

Maintain grace under pressure. Know right from wrong. And have courage.

LINCOLN PRINCIPLES

★ Refrain from reading attacks upon yourself so you won't be provoked.

★ Don't be terrified by an excited populace and hindered from speaking your honest sentiments.

★ It's not entirely safe to allow a misrepresentation to go uncontradicted.

★ Remember that *truth* is generally the best vindication against slander.

★ Do the very best you know how—the very best you can—and keep doing so until the end.

★ If you yield to even one false charge, you may open yourself up to other unjust attacks.

★ If both factions or neither shall harass you, you will probably be about right. Beware of being assailed by one and praised by the other.

★ The probability that you may fall in the struggle ought not to deter you from the support of a cause you believe to be just.

Take *time* and think *well* upon this subject. Nothing valuable can be lost by taking time.

Delay is ruining us.

Time is everything. Please act in view of this.

Make haste slowly.

Lincoln giving seemingly contradictory advice to different followers in different situations (March 1861–July 1862)

7 / *Be a Master of Paradox*

Although Abraham Lincoln has not generally been regarded as a leader with charisma, there are many observations that support the theory that he did, indeed, possess a certain amount of that magical quality. For example, whenever he went into the field the troops greeted him with wild, sometimes frenzied cheering. He was the recipient of a spontaneous reception and demonstration at the conclusion of his Cooper Institute Address in New York City. When he left Springfield for Washington in 1861 more than 1,000 people showed up unexpectedly at the train station, prompting his moving and unrehearsed Farewell Address. And there are numerous accounts of people instinctively crowding around him and reacting with excitement when he approached. The tremendous outpouring of grief after his death is further testament to his immense popularity. Moreover, part of the "Lincoln Myth" bestowed on him a certain amount of saintly virtue. He was a father figure to many people of his day. Indeed, his name, Abraham, literally means father, and, like his height, may have had a psychological effect on followers.

And Lincoln is charismatic even in death. Mention of his name still generates great emotion. Today he has a tremendous following that spans all walks of life, all professions, all around the globe. James MacGregor Burns could have been writing about Abraham Lincoln when he discussed the role of charisma in leadership:

> The term itself means the endowment of divine grace, but [it is not clear] whether this gift of grace was a quality possessed by leaders independent of society or a quality dependent on its recognition by followers. The term has taken on a number of different but overlapping meanings: leaders' magical qualities; an emotional bond between leader and led; dependence on a father figure by the masses; popular assumptions that a leader is powerful, omniscient, and virtuous; imputation of enormous supernatural power to leaders (or secular power, or both); and simply popular support for a leader that verges on love.

It is difficult, and sometimes paradoxical, to think of Abraham Lincoln as a man who possessed charisma in much the same way as, say, John F. Kennedy did. After all, this is the same stoic-faced individual we see in old photographs; the never-smiling man of the statues and busts; the man who dressed in black, dull, ill-fitting clothes and rarely combed his hair. But "paradox" is a most appropriate description for not only Lincoln the man but Lincoln the leader. There were, in fact, numerous paradoxes in Lincoln's leadership style. For instance, he tended to be strikingly flexible while at the same time a model of consistency.

During the four years of his presidency, Lincoln was remarkably consistent. Early in his first administration the president directed and encouraged his cabinet members to be consistent in their choices for political appointments, to be sure their actions met with the public's needs and opinions. Consistency became one of Lincoln's subtle trademarks and one of the main cogs in the machinery of his administration. Such dependability from a leader inspires trust and naturally makes people feel more comfortable on a day-to-day basis. Lincoln was consistent in how he treated people, and how he made assignments and promotions; consistent in his interaction with his cabinet members and generals; and consistent in how he administered and managed the government and its war machine. He ordered military appointments and commissions only "if it can consistently be done"; he released boys from military service if, in the discretion of the commanding officer, "you think it is not inconsistent with the public interest." Lincoln even used the "consistency" rationale to justify his running for a second term: "I have not permitted myself, gentlemen, to conclude that I am the best man in the country," he once said to the National Urban League, "but I am reminded, in this connection, of a story of an old Dutch farmer, who remarked to a companion once that 'it was not best to swap horses when crossing streams.'"

Yet, while being a model of consistency, Lincoln was also uncommonly flexible. He was a leader who would not and did not limit himself. "My policy is to have no policy," he'd say. "I shall not surrender this game leaving any available card unplayed." Lincoln would always leave "an opportunity for a change of mind."

He'd committed himself to doing whatever it took to preserve, protect, and defend the Constitution of the United States, which to him meant keeping the country together. In a letter to Horace Greeley, written in 1862, the president described his view of this "*official* duty," which included an unbending devotion to flexibility:

I shall do *less* whenever I shall believe what I am doing

hurts the cause, and I shall do *more* whenever I shall believe doing more will help the cause. I shall try to correct errors when shown to be errors; and I shall adopt new views so fast as they shall appear to be true views.

Lincoln's adept handling of paradox has been confirmed by recent leadership studies as an essential skill for all leaders. Tom Peters, in his book *Thriving On Chaos*, recommended promoting those individuals who deal best with paradox. "Managers at all levels," he wrote, "must come to grips with paradoxes that have set conventional management wisdom on its ear." He offered "tips for that paradox-loving manager who must be the leader of the future: be out and about; only by being at the front line will you be able to feel the pace, the progress, and the problems where it counts; listen and provide listening forums; learn to love and laud failures; and preach speedy horizontal communication."

Lincoln showed his mastery of paradox by skillfully providing a rock-solid, stable government as a foundation for the nation's security, while at the same time personally instituting massive amounts of change. He coupled this chief paradox with many other seemingly contradictory approaches that all leaders, in every walk of life, must master to be successful. Here are just some of the paradoxes that are easily identifiable in Lincoln's leadership style:

★ He was charismatic yet unassuming.
★ He was consistent yet flexible.
★ He was the victim of vast amounts of slander and malice, yet he was also immensely popular with the troops.
★ He was trusting and compassionate, yet could also be demanding and tough.
★ He was a risk-taker and innovative, yet patient and calculating.

★ He seemed to have a "revolving door" of generals whom he often removed and replaced; yet, in reality, he gave them ample time and support to produce results.

★ He claimed not to have controlled events, that his policy was to have no policy when, in actuality, he did control events to a very large degree by being aggressive, taking charge, and being extraordinarily decisive.

One naturally wonders how Lincoln could possibly have managed all of these amazing inconsistencies during so trying a time in American history. Yet not only did he manage them, he mastered these paradoxes in so formidable a manner that, by being more often proactive than reactive, he actually controlled the outcome of events. While Lincoln was able to capitalize on his own strengths, he was also able to recognize his shortcomings, compensate for them, and play down his darker side.

All human beings have their weaknesses, but not all of us realize them, come to grips with them, or offset their negative impact. As a group whose primary endeavor is interacting with other people, leaders *must* accomplish the paradoxical task of managing their darker sides. Subordinates look for their bosses to be positive, in good humor, and cheerful. They aren't supposed to be emotional or have bad days. But leaders are human, too, and when they are in a lousy mood and snap at a subordinate, it can have a devastating effect.

How did Lincoln control the more negative aspects of his character, such as anger and frustration? Though once in a while he would blow up and lose his temper, he usually did it in private. To avoid such a display, Lincoln would sit down and write lengthy letters that generally did not send. They served as ways to release his pent-up emotional feelings.

Recall that he drafted a statement refuting McClellan's slanderous remarks concerning the "Antietam episode" but would not allow Ward Lamon to deliver it. And to Gen.

George Meade after Gettysburg Lincoln wrote a scathing letter discussing his dissatisfaction with the general for not engaging Lee's army and for allowing their escape into Virginia. "I was in such deep distress myself," he wrote, "that I could not restrain some expression of it." But Lincoln would not send this letter either. In fact, on the outside envelope he later wrote: "To Gen. Meade, never sent, or signed."

Near the conclusion of William Rosecrans's victory at Chattanooga, Tennessee, in September 1863, Lincoln once vented his anger in the presence of the War Department's Telegraph Office staff. Upon hearing that Gen. Ambrose Burnside had headed his army in the direction of Jonesboro rather than to Chattanooga in support of Rosecrans, Lincoln is reported to have bounced his stovepipe hat off the floor and cried, "Damn Jonesboro!" This was the only time anyone in that office would ever hear the president swear. But Lincoln was terribly angered. Burnside, he thought, had disobeyed a direct order and had not followed through on what he said he was going to do. So, characteristically, Lincoln sat down and wrote his general a chiding letter: "It makes me doubt whether I am awake or dreaming," he stated. "I have been struggling for ten days, first through Gen. Halleck, and then directly, to get you to go assist Gen. Rosecrans in an extremity, and you have repeatedly declared you would do it, and yet you steadily move the contrary way."

Once again, however, Lincoln simply wrote on the back of the letter "Not sent." He felt better for having released his negative feelings, but probably realized that to chew out Burnside at that point in time would serve no useful purpose.

Lincoln usually exhibited his darker sides only in private; sometime later, after cooling off, he would again address the problem, in a less emotional frame of mind. But Lincoln's primary goal was to not lose his temper at all, or at least to minimize the times he would do so. His strategy was simply to not put himself in that position, to *avoid conflict* wherever possible. "Let minor differences, and personal preferences, if there be such; go to the winds," he once said. In 1860, Lincoln wrote to Cornelius F. McNeill: "I wish no explanation made to our enemies. What they want is a squabble and a fuss; and that they can have if we explain; and they can not have if we don't." And in 1864, the president lectured Assistant Secretary of the Navy Gustavus V. Fox about conflict: "You have more of that feeling of personal resentment than I," Lincoln told him. "Perhaps I may have too little of it, but I never thought it paid. A man has not time to spend half his life in quarrels. If any man ceases to attack me, I never remember the past against him."

In October 1863, Lincoln delivered a stern reprimand to Capt. James M. Cutts, a young officer whose chief offense was engaging in conflict and verbally abusing a brother officer. Lincoln told Cutts not to quarrel at all:

> No man resolved to make the most of himself, can spare time for personal contention. Still less can he afford to take all the consequences, including the vitiating of his temper, and the loss of self-control. Yield larger things to which you can show no more than equal right; and yield lesser ones, though clearly your own. Better give your path to a dog, than be bitten by him in contesting for the right. Even killing the dog would not cure the bite.

In the many schools of leadership, it is not often that a prospective supervisor will be advised to simply avoid quarreling. In fact, rarely are seminars offered on the more negative aspects of the leader's job. More often, such sessions tend to focus on the positive, "can do" viewpoint. But the plain fact of the matter is that, for any person to successfully lead others, he or she must deal with reality and be ready to accept the fact that leadership, at times, can bring out the worst in us. And understanding, as well as coming to grips with the darker side of your personality, is key to dealing with real-life situations.

Lincoln was able to do it, and so can contemporary leaders, who can learn from his skill. He managed his darker side by displaying his outrage only in private, writing long letters to vent his anger and emotion, avoiding conflict wherever possible, and never quarreling over insignificant matters.

But keeping one's darker side under control is only one component of mastering paradox. New leaders in today's fast-paced business climate must be ready to deal with complex situations that require a variety of different approaches. In some instances, it will be necessary to make quick decisions and take risks so as not to miss important opportunities. In other cases, a conservative and patient approach may be necessary to more thoroughly research a venture.

Corporate leaders of the future will have to provide employee security while also encouraging an environment for risk taking. At times it will seem like walking a delicate tightrope. But, in reality, it is nothing more than the simple understanding that each person, and each situation, is different and should be handled uniquely, in some cases with completely opposite styles. In many ways, mastering paradox is nothing more than having good common sense.

LINCOLN PRINCIPLES

★ Make consistency one of the main cogs in the machinery of your corporation.

★ Remember that it is not best to swap horses when crossing steams.

★ Don't surrender the game leaving any available card unplayed.

★ Do *less* whenever you believe what you are doing hurts the cause, and do *more* whenever you believe doing more will help the cause. Try to correct errors when they are shown to be errors; and adopt new views so fast as they appear to be true views.

★ You must come to grips with the paradox of providing employee security while also encouraging an environment for risk-taking.

★ When you are in deep distress and cannot restrain some expression of it, sit down and write out a harsh letter venting your anger. But don't send it.

★ Make no explanation to your enemies. What they want is a squabble and a fuss; and that they can have if you explain, and they can not have if you don't.

★ Avoid major conflict in the form of quarrels and arguments. You simply don't have time for it.

PART III
ENDEAVOR

Some single mind must be master, else there will be no agreement in anything. . . .

> Part of Lincoln's firm stance regarding new elections in the State of Arkansas (February 17, 1864)

8 / *Exercise a Strong Hand— Be Decisive*

Abraham Lincoln is generally regarded as the first modern president in several respects. While he is most famous for freeing the slaves and preserving the federal Union, he also greatly expanded the limits of American presidential authority and power. In fact, even though it was not his original intention, he practically redefined the presidency while, at the same time, notably revising the American constitutional system.

Faced with the potential dissolution of the Union and overthrow of the government, Lincoln acted and reacted by creating new limits of authority and leadership under the pressure of dire civil strife. The nation, after all, was undergoing a civil war—something that no previous president had been forced to deal with and something that the Founding Fathers had not specifically provided for in the Constitution. Circumstances forced Lincoln to be innovative, and he justified his expansion of authority by invoking a new interpretation of the presidential oath regarding the Constitution itself:

> My oath . . . imposed upon me the duty of preserving, by every indispensable means, that government—that nation—of which that Constitution was the organic law. Was it possible to lose the nation, and yet preserve the Constitution? By general law life *and* limb must be protected; yet often a limb must be amputated to save a life; but a life is never wisely given to save a limb. I felt that measures, otherwise unconstitutional, might become lawful, by becoming indispensable to the preservation of the Constitution, through the preservation of the nation.

Now, if this passage, written by Lincoln to Albert Hodges in April 1864, were to be read by someone who did not have a general concept of his broad assumption of authority and power, the question might arise: "What did Lincoln *do?*" A better question might be, however, "What did Lincoln *not* do?" In truth, he was so decisive that he left virtually no stone unturned. He took advantage of nearly every situation at hand. Confusion, desperation, and urgency all combined to give Lincoln the perfect opportunity to act. The nation needed a leader's strong hand, and Lincoln provided it.

Within weeks of the firing on Fort Sumter, the president issued a call for troops, one of at least ten such orders he would make over the next four years. (Lincoln was the first president to enact conscription, on August 4, 1862, as a way of raising an army to fight a war.) He issued proclamations directing a blockade of the Confederate states from Virginia to Texas. He declared martial law by suspending the writ of *habeas corpus,* which allowed the military to make arrests without specific charges. This one act alone overshadowed his primary purpose, which was to protect the nation from spies and traitors, in that it created such widespread dissent among citizens and other government officials that it almost backfired. Chief

Justice of the Supreme Court Roger B. Taney assailed Lincoln on the matter, claiming that only Congress had the right to suspend *habeas corpus*. The Democratic party and its friendly press had a field day labeling the president a dictator and a tyrant. But through it all Lincoln stood firm, and he continued to suspend the writ as he saw the need. Lincoln's interpretation of presidential war powers stretched the meaning of the Constitution to its limit, and future presidents would cite his actions as justification for their own.

Early in his first term, Lincoln was constantly pressured by key advisers to capitulate to the South's demands to avoid a bloody conflict. On one occasion, he was advised by a Virginian to surrender all forts and property in the Southern states. Lincoln immediately rejected the option by telling Aesop's parable of the lion and the woodman's daughter:

> A lion was very much in love with a woodman's daughter. The fair maid referred him to her father and the lion applied for the girl. The father replied: "Your teeth are too long." So the lion went to a dentist and had them extracted. Returning, he asked for his bride. "No," said the woodman, "your claws are too long." Going back to the dentist, he had them drawn. Then he returned to claim his bride, and the woodman, seeing that he was unarmed, beat out his brains.

"May it not be so with me," concluded the president, "if I give up all that is asked?"

The decision to resupply Fort Sumter, rather than evacuate or commence hostilities, turned out to be a shrewd move on Lincoln's part. Not only was it consistent with the strategy he outlined in his inaugural address but, once the Confederates fired on the fort, the president was provided with an opportunity that justified strong, decisive action. It was the start of the Civil War, and public opinion in the North clamored for immediate retaliation. Don E. Fehrenbacher, a prominent

Lincoln scholar, has noted that because it *was* an act of war ". . . it provided a constitutional basis for vigorous executive action that had hitherto been lacking. And, because, coming as it did when Congress was not in session, the Fort Sumter episode gave Lincoln the opportunity to seize the initiative from the legislative branch—an initiative that he never relinquished." It is also significant to note that the president did not call Congress into special session until July 4, 1861, thereby giving him almost three months to act on his own.

During his administration, Lincoln set a precedent of directing the expenditure of money without the official approval of Congress. For example, he ordered Secretary of the Treasury Chase to give $2 million to three New York businessmen for the purpose of aiding the military buildup. He ordered the Navy to purchase twenty new ships and appropriated money for Stanton and Seward to use in carrying out the suspension of the writ of *habeas corpus*. He also allocated money to "encourage immigration."

In running the administration's war effort, Lincoln did everything from asking Gen. Winfield Scott to "make short, comprehensive reports to me" to completely revamping and reorganizing the American military command system. He issued numerous formal "War Orders" in an effort to get his generals moving, and he revoked orders and proclamations issued by his generals that had not been approved by him. On one hand, Lincoln wanted his generals to take action on their own; on the other, he would not allow them to dictate policy, which he deemed should come only from him.

The president did not always take kindly to people who were not involved in the day-to-day operations of the government making demands upon him or telling him how he should run the war effort. But, rather than harshly turning away such individuals, Lincoln would ease them out of his office with a short, appropriate anecdote. For example, when a delegation of politicians from the West invaded his office making excited demands, he simply shut them off by responding:

Gentlemen, suppose all the property you were worth
was in gold and this you had placed in the hands of
[one man] to carry across the Niagara River on a rope.
Would you shake the cable and keep shouting at him:
"Stand up a little straighter; stoop a little more, go a little
faster, go a little slower, lean a little more to the south?"
No, you would hold your breath, as well as your tongue,
and keep your hands off until he got safely over.

The Government is carrying an enormous weight.
Untold treasure is in their hands. Don't badger them.
Keep silence and we will get you safely across.

On September 22, 1862, President Lincoln did something
that he felt he had very little constitutional authority to do: He
issued the Preliminary Emancipation Proclamation. At the advice
of Secretary Seward, Lincoln timed its issuance to occur after a
major Union victory, which, by chance, turned out to include the
bloodiest single day of the Civil War, McClellan's victory at
Antietam, Maryland. The document, which was to become the
most controversial and the most important of his presidency,
proclaimed that all slaves living in any state not in the Union by
January 1, 1863, would be "henceforward, and forever free."
When Secretary Chase suggested to Lincoln that he extend
emancipation to other areas, the president refused to consider it:

The original proclamation, has no constitutional or
legal justification, except as a military measure. The
exemptions were made because the military necessity
did not apply to the exempted localities. Nor does that
necessity apply to them now any more than it did then.
If I take the step must I not do so, without the
argument of military necessity, and so without any
argument except the one that I think the measure
politically expedient and morally right? Would I not
thus give up all footing upon Constitution or law?

accurately surmised that any freeing of the slaves
ere would alienate the border states, and the Union could
not afford to lose any more states than it had already lost. Part of
the "military necessity" justification for the proclamation was the
inference that freed blacks could be used in the armed forces. This
bold decision resulted in a substantial increase in the number of
Northern troops. However, on February 1, 1865, not three
months before his death, Lincoln approved and signed the
resolution submitting the Thirteenth Amendment (Abolition of
Slavery) to the states for ratification.

In helping to restore the Confederate states and their citizens
to the Union, Lincoln was resourceful and explicit in taking
decisive executive action. In his annual message to Congress of
December 8, 1863, the president outlined his proposed "ten
percent" plan whereby any seceded state, in order to return to the
Union, was required to have no less than ten percent of its
citizens who voted in 1860 take an oath of allegiance to the
United States. Upon doing so, the states could then organize
their own government and could have senators and representatives readmitted to Congress, provided they agreed to recognize
the abolishment of slavery and educate newly emancipated slaves.
The oath, in essence, also offered amnesty to nearly everyone
who participated in the rebellion.

Initially Lincoln's plan of reconstruction received favorable
reviews. Most of Congress, however, thought it a bit too
lenient, and in 1864 they conceived and passed the harsher
Wade-Davis Bill, which required a "fifty percent" number
swearing allegiance. Knowing that obtaining such a majority
of citizens would be difficult, the president, on July 4,
pocket-vetoed the bill and, just four days later, released a
statement explaining his actions. He found the Wade-Davis
Bill "to be inflexibly committed to [a] single plan of restoration," and he did not wish to "set aside the already adopted
and installed governments in Arkansas and Louisiana." In
issuing this statement clarifying his reasons for not signing the
bill, Lincoln was doing something that most modern presi-

dents are now forced to do: He was explaining himself to the American people through the press. The president, Lincoln believed, was a servant of and answered to the people; as such, the public had a right to know why he made the decision.

Lincoln could also be decisive and tough with his direct subordinates when he was forced to do so. Several members of the president's cabinet proved to be quite difficult. One problem individual was Secretary of the Treasury Salmon P. Chase, who was obsessed with becoming president himself, so much so that everyone in Washington knew it, including Lincoln. One might question Lincoln's judgment in retaining Chase when his motives were so obvious. But Chase was a competent, able administrator, and Lincoln needed him to help run the government and raise money to pay for the war effort.

Lincoln often accepted the aggravation and exasperation caused by subordinates if they did their jobs competently. Unfortunately, Chase would continually precipitate problems for the president. The two often clashed over policy matters, large and small. Chase demanded complete control over appointments to the Treasury Department, and there were a great many such placements. For the most part, Lincoln let Chase have his way and seldom interfered. However, on two occasions when the president did step in and overrule Treasury appointments, Chase submitted his resignation in protest. He also resigned on one occasion when, in February 1864, a press circular prematurely exposed his movement to replace Lincoln as the Republican presidential nominee. When asked what he was going to do about Chase's ambition to become president, Lincoln responded with a story of how he and his brother were once plowing corn with a lazy horse:

> On reaching the end of the furrow, I found an enormous chin-fly fastened upon [the horse], and knocked him off. My brother asked me what I did that for. I told him I didn't want the old horse bitten in that way. "Why," said my brother, "that's all that made him go."

Now, if Mr. Chase has a Presidential chin-fly biting him, I'm not going to knock him off, if it will only make his department go.

In all, Salmon P. Chase formally offered to resign four times over the course of the administration. He used this tactic at times as a ploy to get his way with the president. However, the last time he did it, on June 29, 1864, Lincoln surprised him—he accepted his resignation and forced him to leave the administration. At this point, their relationship had been reduced to one where they communicated mostly by formal, frigid memorandums, and Lincoln simply had had enough. The next day, he sent Chase this final memo:

EXECUTIVE MANSION

Washington

June 30, 1864

Hon. Salmon P. Chase

My dear Sir.

Your resignation of the office of Secretary of the Treasury, sent me yesterday, is accepted. Of all I have said in commendation of your ability and fidelity, I have nothing to unsay; and yet you and I have reached a point of mutual embarrassment in our official relation which it seems can not be overcome, or longer sustained, consistently with the public service.

Your Obt. Servt.
A. Lincoln

When word got out that Lincoln had dismissed his secretary of the treasury, Chase's friends in the Senate stormed the White House to demand justification. The president, however, remained firm in his decision. He specified the former secretary's inflexibility regarding appointments and spoke of their unworkable relationship. Lincoln told the senators that he had no choice, under the circumstances, but to let him go. The next day, the president astonished everyone by appointing one of Chase's strongest supporters, Sen. William P. Fessenden, to be the new secretary of the treasury. Lincoln had made an immediate political decision, in part to pacify the liberal Republican opposition to Chase's dismissal.

As for Chase, who thought that his public service career was at an end, Lincoln appointed him to be the new chief justice of the Supreme Court. When protests came against this move, Lincoln responded publicly by saying:

> Chase is a very able man. He is a very ambitious man and I think on the subject of the presidency a little insane. He has not always behaved very well lately and people say to me, "Now is the time to *crush him out*." Well, I'm not in favor of crushing anybody out! If there is anything that a man can do and do it well, I say let him do it. Give him a chance.

Privately, however, Lincoln may have been having second thoughts, because he was later reported to have remarked that he "would rather have swallowed his buckhorn chair than to have nominated Chase." In an ironic twist of fate, it was Salmon P. Chase who administered the oath of office to Abraham Lincoln upon the occasion of his second inaugural.

The president also surprised his postmaster-general, Montgomery Blair, on September 23, 1864, with a directive that stated in part: "You have generously said to me more than once, that whenever your resignation could be a relief to me, it was at my disposal. The time has come." Lincoln removed

Blair partly because of the secretary's denunciation of Chase, Seward, and Stanton in public, and partly because he was indiscreet and argued openly with the radical Republican members of Congress on policy matters. With the election of 1864 nearing, Lincoln concluded that Blair must go for him to consolidate support within his own party.

Lincoln had the will and the ability to make tough decisions when necessary. And he did not hesitate once he was convinced that swift action had to take place. However, it is certain that for every crucial decision of his administration Lincoln thought things out well in advance. In fact, he employed a classic decision-making sequence of events that began with an understanding of all the facts that were involved, often obtaining this information himself by venturing into the field. Lincoln would also consider a variety of possible solutions and the consequences of each. Finally, he would assure himself that any action taken would be consistent with his administrative and personal policy objectives. And then he would effectively communicate his decision and implement it.

What would have been the consequences had Lincoln not been decisive? We can only shudder at the thought. We certainly recognize that his decisiveness enacted extraordinary change. He literally changed attitudes, behaviors, and the way people lived their lives. He altered the face of the nation forever by abolishing the institution of slavery and not allowing the South to secede. And, what is more, he actually *intended* to do both, which, almost by definition, makes him a great leader. He set his goals, preached his vision, and accomplished his mission.

Like Lincoln, the best, most decisive leaders are those who have a set purpose and the self-confidence to accomplish that objective. But effective visions and noble goals can be made worthless without solid decision-making leadership, especially in today's fast-paced, competitive business environment where decisions are almost never simply black and white. Often, all the information is not available and an important decision must be made by a certain deadline. Short-term solutions are frequently at odds with long-term goals. Sometimes the leader makes the right choice even though it may not be immediately obvious. Sometimes he is wrong, and sometimes he chooses to compromise, which can be a major decision in itself. Many contemporary leaders view negotiation as a lack of decisiveness, but they forget the words of John F. Kennedy, who reminded us that "compromise need not mean cowardice."

Business executives know that it is sometimes difficult to implement decisions that have major impact on an organization. Willingness to make change is not easy to come by, and bureaucratic stumbling blocks are often seemingly impossible to overcome. But decisions must be made, and they must be consistent for any organization to be successful. Consider for a moment what a company is like *without* effective decisiveness: Nothing happens and opportunities are lost. People wander about aimlessly, aggressive employees become frustrated, and lethargic employees are not motivated.

But in a corporation *with* decisive leaders the atmosphere is dynamic and vibrant. People move with a spring in their step and purpose in their direction. Opportunity seeks out the company, and the well-focused firm—one backed by solid vision and well thought out goals—almost always succeeds.

Abraham Lincoln understood that executive decision-making is not simply a string of individual orders. Rather, it is more of a continuous, uninterrupted process that is similar to the beating of a heart that sends blood throughout a body. Without it there is no life.

Competent executive decision-making is crucial in any organization. Abraham Lincoln knew it. And because of his extraordinary decisiveness, he was able to make policy, produce change, and win the war.

LINCOLN PRINCIPLES

★ An entire organization is never wisely sacrificed to avoid losing one or two small parts.

★ Take advantage of confusion, desperation, and urgency to exercise strong leadership.

★ Seize the initiative and never relinquish it.

★ Don't give up all your key points of strength or the competition may "beat out your brains."

★ Never let your immediate subordinate take action upon *your* responsibility without consulting you first.

★ If you have a subordinate who has a presidential chin-fly biting him, don't knock it off.

★ When making a decision, understand the facts, consider various solutions and their consequences, make sure that the decision is consistent with your objectives, and effectively communicate your judgment.

★ Remember that compromise does not mean cowardice.

★ Try ballots first; when ballots don't work, use bullets.

Now, the undertaking being a success, the honor is all yours; for I believe none of us went farther than to acquiesce. . . . But what next? I suppose it will be safer if I leave Gen. Grant and yourself to decide.

Part of Lincoln's response to General Sherman for his "Christmas gift"—the capture of Savannah (December 26, 1864)

9 / *Lead by Being Led*

There is much evidence to indicate that Lincoln, largely through his extraordinary assertiveness, stood alone when it came to making major decisions during his presidency. Even though he often conferred with his advisers on important matters, using them as sounding boards, it is clear that Lincoln made most crucial decisions during his term in office. He alone bore the responsibility and would answer to the American people for his actions. While he often disavowed taking the lead in determining the nation's course of action (he once said, "I claim not to have controlled events, but confess plainly that events have controlled me"), it is also clear that Lincoln skillfully steered the ship of state through the perilous waters of the Civil War. It was Lincoln who led the way while at times giving the impression that he was, rather, following the lead of his subordinates. And here, in essence, is one of the marks of his true leadership genius. As Lao Tzu said: "Fail to honor people, they fail to honor you. But of a good leader, who talks little, when his work is done, his aim fulfilled, they will all say, 'We did this ourselves'."

Lincoln also had the enviable quality of being able to listen to people and be guided by them without being threatened himself. He possessed the open-mindedness and flexibility necessary for worthwhile leadership. Frequently he would listen to his subordinates' suggestions and recommendations. If they made sense, and if their course of action matched his own ideas, he would let them proceed with the knowledge and belief that it was their idea. However, if he was uncomfortable with what was being suggested, Lincoln would focus, direct, or point his people to what he viewed as the proper path. But rather than ordering or dictating, Lincoln refined his ability to direct others by implying, hinting, or suggesting.

The shrewdness and subtlety with which Lincoln guided people has not generally been recognized. Often his actions seemed so innocent that contemporaries and subordinates had no inkling that Lincoln's hand was involved in the circuitous changing of events. One famous case in point involved the president's adept handling of Secretary of the Treasury Salmon P. Chase's attempts to discredit William Seward in late 1862. Chase was jealous of Seward's influence with the president and of their close friendship. He felt that it was he who should be the chief adviser in the cabinet; in fact, in 1864 he worked behind the scenes in an attempt to wrest the Republican nomination from Lincoln. Chase had complained to influential Republican senators that Seward exerted undue influence on the president, that he was inept at handling foreign affairs, and that he was the cause of all the problems at the executive level of the government.

After the Confederate victory over General Burnside at Fredericksburg, Virginia, the senators were overly distraught and subsequently met in caucuses to discuss Seward's position in the cabinet. They decided to send a delegation of nine to the White House to urge Lincoln to dismiss the secretary of state and reorganize the cabinet. At their meeting, on December 18, 1862, they accused Seward of endless wrongdoing and told Lincoln that they had it on good authority that the president often failed to consult all members of his cabinet when important decisions were made. Lincoln asked them to return the following night. Until then he would consider their concerns and demands. In the meantime, Seward, incensed over the entire episode, submitted his letter of resignation to the president, who did not act immediately upon it but slipped it in one of his coat pockets.

Lincoln, too, was upset over the sequence of events and the possible repercussions. He did not want Seward to go, nor did he wish to reorganize any part of his cabinet. He especially didn't want Congress dictating to him how he should administer his cabinet and make decisions. He also correctly deduced that Chase was at the center of all this turmoil. After much private deliberation Lincoln decided to call all parties (except Seward) together to resolve the situation and force Secretary Chase into a corner.

The next evening he summoned his cabinet to a special session where he explained all that had happened the night before. When the senators returned to the White House for their scheduled meeting, Lincoln assembled everyone in the same room and asked that all matters of dispute be resolved before anyone left. All the participants were caught off guard. The senators did not know that the cabinet was going to be present, nor did the cabinet realize what Lincoln had secretly planned. Chase was especially distressed. If he were to support all that the senators had asserted, his cabinet colleagues and the president were sure to realize that he was the catalyst to all the dissent. Chase was forced to agree that Lincoln had consulted the cabinet on every important decision, that they were generally in agreement, and that Seward acted properly and honestly in the administration of his duties as secretary of state. As a result of this meeting, organized and run exclusively by Lincoln, the Republican senators and Chase were thoroughly embarrassed and humiliated. Chase was exposed as a fraud never to be trusted again, and all charges against Seward were dropped. Lincoln obtained the results he wanted while seeming to be almost naive in his actions. He simply got everybody together to talk it out!

The following day, in the presence of Secretary of War Stanton and Secretary of the Navy Gideon Welles, Chase tendered *his* resignation. "Where is it? Let me have it!" insisted the president. Then Stanton, probably surprised by Lincoln's reaction, impulsively offered his own resignation. "No," said Lincoln waving him away, "I don't want yours!" But, he took Chase's and, as a result, now had *two* letters of resignation, one in each of his coat pockets. A short time later, the exhilarated president told a visitor in private that he "could ride now," because, "I've got a pumpkin at each end of my bag."

So what's the lesson to be learned from this episode? Many corporate leaders will recognize Lincoln's method because it is an often-used technique. They get all the members of feuding departments together, lock them in a conference room— sometimes on a Saturday—and compel them to stay together until peace is made. Frequently, getting people together can avoid destructive thinking that tends to build on people's misgivings and apprehensions about others and their departments.

Lincoln's approach was similar. Rather than order the disputing parties to stop bickering and get on with their business, or simply announcing his support for Seward and condemning Chase and the senators, Lincoln chose to try and let the individuals involved work out their differences by bringing them together and guiding their dialogue. Had he dictated, they may have accepted his authority with great resentment. But the problem would not have gone away. It would have lingered and festered. By gathering the disputing parties, Lincoln let his subordinates lead themselves out of the mess.

Another habit employed by Lincoln in his strategy of

"leading while being led" was to always give credit where credit was due and, conversely, to accept responsibility when things went wrong. Not only did this satisfy Lincoln's need for honesty, integrity, and human dignity; it also gave his subordinates the correct perception that *they* were, in many ways, doing the leading, not Lincoln. If nothing else, it made them feel good about their jobs. It also encouraged innovation and risk taking because they knew that if they failed, Lincoln would not blame them.

When a subordinate did a good job, Lincoln praised, complimented, and rewarded the individual. On the other hand, he shouldered responsibility when mistakes were made. The president, for example, readily accepted responsibility for the battles lost during the Civil War. He tried to let his generals know that if they failed, he too failed. The loss of the second battle of Bull Run, for example, created a great deal of anger in Washington, most of it directed at Gen. George McClellan because he failed to provide field commander John Pope with appropriate support. It was generally believed at the time that McClellan wanted Pope to fail. As a result, several angered cabinet officers signed a letter of protest condemning McClellan for his conduct during the battle and demanded his dismissal. Lincoln chose instead to appoint McClellan to the command of the forces in Washington. The cabinet members first heard of the appointment together in session with the president, and an infuriated Secretary of War Stanton exclaimed that no such order had been issued from the War Department. Lincoln then responded somewhat calmly, "No, Mr. Secretary, the order was mine; and I will be responsible for it to the country." Lincoln felt that McClellan should not have to bear the entire burden for the loss. He also felt that there were no other officers who were better suited to the command. So, after the battle, he appointed McClellan at the risk of having his entire cabinet resign.

Throughout the war Lincoln continued to accept public responsibility for battles lost or opportunities missed. In the days following the battle of Gettysburg, for example, the president was distressed at General Meade's delay in pursuing Robert E. Lee before his army made it back across the Potomac River. Well after the battle, in an attempt to spur the general into active confrontation with Lee, the president sent him a letter through General Halleck urging an immediate attack. "If General Meade can now attack him on a field no worse than equal for us," said Lincoln, "and will do so with all the skill and courage, which he, his officers, and men possess, the honor will be his if he succeeds, and the blame may be mine if he fails."

And within a few weeks after Ulysses Grant captured Vicksburg, Lincoln sent his victorious general a personal letter of commendation in which he admitted that he had initially questioned Grant's strategy but now praised him for his efforts:

> I do not remember that you and I ever met personally. I write this now as a grateful acknowledgment for the almost inestimable service you have done the country. I wish to say a word further. When you first reached the vicinity of Vicksburg . . . I never had any faith, except a general hope that you knew better than I that the expedition could succeed. . . . I feared it was a mistake. I now wish to make the personal acknowledgment that you were right, and I was wrong.

Why was it important that Lincoln send this letter to Grant? Because, in doing so, he was directly informing his general that the president and the government genuinely appreciated and approved of his actions. This would spur Grant to continue his aggressive style, which, of course, is exactly what Lincoln wanted. Indirectly, Lincoln was also saying that he would not take credit for the general's successes, which appealed to Grant's ego and sense of self-worth.

During the war, Lincoln sent similar letters to generals who had taken the initiative and achieved distinction. On December 26, 1864, he wrote to General Sherman:

> Many, many, thanks for your Christmas gift—the capture of Savannah. When you were about leaving Atlanta for the Atlantic coast, I was *anxious,* if not fearful. . . . Now, the undertaking being a success, the honor is all yours; for I believe none of us went farther than to acquiesce. . . . But what next? I suppose it will be safer if I leave Gen. Grant and yourself to decide.

Sherman's response to this communiqué is a perfect illustration of why it is important for contemporary leaders to emulate Lincoln's style.

> I am gratified at the receipt of your letter, . . . especially to observe that you appreciate the division I made of my army. . . . Should I venture too much and happen to lose I shall bespeak your charitable influence. . . . I am ready [to move again] as soon as I can learn of . . . your preference of objectives.

Sherman was more willing to act on his own now. All Lincoln had to do at this point was to provide some broad guidance, and Sherman would do the rest. If leaders do enough of this—if they praise good work and encourage more of the same—then eventually they will be able to relax and let their subordinates do most of the work. And all the leader will have to do is guide them in the proper direction.

Lincoln continued this laudatory style right up to the final days of his life. During his last public address, made to a gathering of people outside the White House on the evening of April 11, 1865, he was filled with modesty for himself and praise for the soldiers who had won the Union victory: "No part of the honor, for plan or execution, is mine," he asserted.

"To General Grant, his skillful officers, and brave men, all belongs."

Any leader can learn from Abraham Lincoln's standard. He had great confidence in his own competence and ability to perform. He was not insecure and did not feel threatened by others. He was flexible, open-minded, and willing to let his subordinates take all the glory for victories.

He gave people the impression that they were leading him. And, in fact, he did give many of his subordinates the lead. But he always exerted some control. He stayed informed of their activity. When their ideas and actions matched his general direction and if he thought there was merit in the means to achieve the overall goal, Lincoln let his subordinates follow through. However, if they were deviating from the proper path, Lincoln guided them back on course. And when the means were inadequate to achieve the goal, he tended to talk them out of it or, when necessary, use his power to overrule. But Lincoln's chief objective was to allow his subordinates to say, "We accomplished this ourselves."

LINCOLN PRINCIPLES

★ If you are a good leader, when your work is done, your aim fulfilled, your people will say, "We did this ourselves."

★ Try not to feel insecure or threatened by your followers.

★ Let disputing parties work out their differences by bringing them together and guiding their dialogue.

★ Always let your subordinates know that the honor will be all theirs if they succeed and the blame will be yours if they fail.

★ Write letters to your subordinates making the personal acknowledgment that they were right and you were wrong.

★ When your subordinates come up with good ideas, let them go ahead and try. But monitor their progress.

★ If your commanders in the field can't be successful, neither can you or your executive staff.

★ Never forget that your organization does not depend on the life of any one individual.

★ The greatest credit should be given to those in your organization who render the hardest work.

I think *Lee's army*, and not *Richmond*, is your true objective point. . . . Fight him when opportunity offers. If he stays where he is, fret him, and fret him.

Lincoln's response to Gen. Joe Hooker, who'd asked for permission to advance on the Confederate capital rather than engage the enemy in combat (June 10, 1863)

10 / *Set Goals and Be Results-Oriented*

Leadership requires aggressive individuals—those who accept a "take charge" role. Leaders, in general, are self-starting and change-oriented. They set a strategic direction and initiate as well as act. They achieve results as opposed to only carrying out activity.

For Lincoln, the need to achieve was more than just a simple inclination; it was an almost uncontrollable obsession. His law partner, William Herndon, noted that he was "always calculating and planning ahead." Lincoln's ambition, wrote Herndon, "was a little engine that knew no rest." In the early years, Lincoln tried several different careers in his quest to succeed in life. He ran a general store, was a postmaster, a surveyor, and eventually a lawyer and politician. His near-compulsive persistence is evident over the course of his entire political career. He was a tireless worker, campaigner, and public speaker.

As a young man, Lincoln tended to be overly ambitious. In 1838, at the age of twenty-nine, delivering one of his more famous speeches to the Young Men's Lyceum of Springfield, Lincoln provided some insight into his own personality when he stated: "Towering genius disdains a beaten path. It seeks regions hitherto unexplored. . . . It *scorns* to tread in the footsteps of *any* predecessor, however illustrious. It thirsts and burns for distinction. . . ."

Lincoln's unyielding drive and aggressiveness was part of his genetic makeup. It was a personal quality, one characteristic of many great leaders. For example, in their early years Roosevelt, Churchill, and Gandhi clearly demonstrated active ambition and an inclination toward attaining a higher station in life. This character trait is a vehicle they all employed to carry out their mission in life.

Without question, Abraham Lincoln "thirsted" and "burned" for distinction. Yet, even though he often became depressed at failure and setbacks, Lincoln developed the enviable ability to persevere and learn from his own failures. Later in life he turned defeat into eventual victory. No endeavor became a hindrance to his overarching goal to achieve. In fact, everything—failures and successes—became stepping-stones to the presidency. In this sense, Lincoln's entire life prepared him for his future executive leadership role.

After his disappointing defeat for the Senate seat won by Stephen A. Douglas in 1858, Lincoln wrote: "The fight must go on. The cause of civil liberty must not be surrendered at the end of one or even one hundred defeats." He wrote to Alexander Sympson of his "abiding faith that we shall beat them in the long run. Step by step the objects of the leaders will become too plain for the people to stand them. . . . I am neither dead nor dying."

Such extraordinary perseverance helped propel Lincoln to the presidency in 1860. As an executive leader, he channeled this intensity toward the personal goal of preserving the United States of America. And it was *progress* toward that goal that Lincoln demanded most, not only of himself, but of those who reported to him.

Establishing goals and gaining their acceptance from subordinates is crucial for effective leadership. Goals unify people, motivate them, focus their talent and energy. Lincoln united his followers with the "corporate mission" of preserving the Union and abolishing slavery, and this objective became more firm and resolute with the onslaught of civil war. Even so, Lincoln realized that the attainment of a successful outcome had to be accomplished in steps. So he constantly set specific short-term goals that his generals and cabinet members could focus on with intent and immediacy. Early in the conflict, he established such strategic objectives as blockading key Southern ports, gaining control of the Mississippi River, and rebuilding and training the military. Throughout the war, he concentrated on the destruction of Lee's army as opposed to the capture of the Confederate capital. And he took one battle at a time rather than trying to win them all at once. Toward the end of hostilities, Lincoln's strategy was to set the stage for peaceful and smooth restoration of the Union. Always, he was working toward achieving goals and objectives. Like all great leaders, Lincoln was driven. He was results-oriented.

In the day-to-day performance of his duties as president, Lincoln worked long, exhaustive hours. Often he'd labor late into the night attending to the vast amount of paperwork that came with the job. Then, rather than retiring, he'd visit the War Department to "see if there is any news," as he would say. He was a positive model for subordinates, displaying remarkable persistence. He attempted to instill the same tenacity and sense of urgency in his generals. "Delay is ruining us," he would write to them. "*Time* is everything!" he would say. His purpose was to be "just and fair," he wrote to New York governor Horatio Seymour, "and yet to not lose time." And when Gen. David Hunter grumbled and complained after being placed in charge of a mere 3,000 men, Lincoln wired back: "Act well your part, there all the honor lies. He who does *something* at the head of one Regiment, will eclipse him who does *nothing* at the head of a hundred."

In the adept and forceful handling of his cabinet officers and generals, Lincoln demonstrated extraordinary perseverance in the face of seemingly insurmountable obstacles and interpersonal clashes. Lincoln did not shun conflict. Instead he resolved dissension among his subordinates in a timely manner, knowing full well that it could serve only to further delay progress. Lincoln realized, as do most leaders, that roadblocks and unresolved conflict simply gum up the works and slow achievement. And he frequently preached this concept to his subordinates. In one instance, when approached by a general for instructions on how to handle a particularly difficult problem, Lincoln told him to use his own best judgment and then related the story of the old farmer who had the task of ploughing a large field laden with many tree stumps!

> It was a terrible place to clear up. But after a while he got a few things growing—here and there a patch of corn, a few hills of beans, and so on. One day a stranger stopped to look at his place and wanted to know how he managed to cultivate so rough a spot. "Well," was the reply, "some of it is pretty rough. The smaller stumps I can generally root out or burn out; but now and then there is [a large one] that bothers me, and there is no other way but to plough around it." Now, General, at such a time as this, troublesome cases are constantly coming up, and the only way to get along at all is to plough around them.

Recent studies in leadership have noted that effective leaders are "reliable and tirelessly persistent" and that they are "the most results-oriented people in the world." Certainly, Lincoln would fit into that mold. He created a contagious enthusiasm among followers by demonstrating a sense of urgency toward attainment of his goals. He wanted them all to be like the dog in one of his favorite anecdotes:

> A man . . . had a small bull-terrier that could whip all the dogs of the neighborhood. The owner of a large dog which the terrier had whipped asked the owner of the terrier how it happened that the terrier whipped every dog he encountered. "That," said the owner of the terrier, "is no mystery to me; your dog and other dogs get half through a fight before they are ready; now, my dog is always mad!"

Contemporary corporate executives constantly worry about how to keep a fire lit under their employees. They must continually motivate, cajole, and persuade. But no one should have to worry about lighting a fire under great leaders. They don't need it if they are like Lincoln. His fire was always burning.

LINCOLN PRINCIPLES

- ★ Unite your followers with a "corporate mission."
- ★ Set specific short-term goals that can be focused on with intent and immediacy by subordinates.
- ★ Those leaders who achieve *something* at the head of one group will eclipse those who do *nothing* at the head of a hundred.
- ★ Sometimes it is better to plough around obstacles rather than to waste time going through them.
- ★ Leave nothing for tomorrow which can be done today.
- ★ Your war will not be won by strategy alone, but more by hard, desperate fighting.
- ★ Your task will neither be done nor attempted unless you watch it every day and hour, and force it.
- ★ Remember that half-finished work generally proves to be labor lost.

I can't spare this man. He fights.

11 / *Keep Searching Until You Find Your "Grant"*

When Abraham Lincoln took office in 1861 he found that the United States was unprepared for war. The country had an insufficient, poorly trained, and poorly equipped army of only 16,000 men under the command of seventy-five-year-old Gen. Winfield Scott. He was too old and physically unable to command in the field, and his theories and strategies of warfare were outdated. What would a contemporary executive leader do when confronted with a situation as severe as this? Sit back? Wait and see if someone came forward to handle the problem? Not so with Lincoln. He took charge.

Because there was such a paucity of military leadership in 1861, Lincoln was forced to formulate the nation's war policy himself. This included everything from drawing up war plans in the War Department offices to directing tactical movements in the field. In the four years that he was in office, Lincoln completely reorganized and redirected the Armed Forces of the United States. In fact, he increased the size of the army so substantially that at the end of the war, General Grant was in command of more than half a million men. Moreover, many of President Lincoln's changes in the American military command system were permanent. And his overall design was later used as something of a blueprint for future reorganization.

At the beginning of his relationship with Winfield Scott, Lincoln treated the aging general with great respect. He called on him at his home or office and often asked his advice on how to conduct the war. They also discussed basic military strategy and organization. General Scott's strategy was to blockade Southern coasts, seize the Mississippi River, keep the Confederates from obtaining its resources, and then to passively sit and wait. He planned no military invasion of the South; instead, he felt that the North should wait for a strong Northern sentiment in the South to overcome talk of secession. This strategy, known as the Anaconda Plan, was immediately rejected by Lincoln. It was essentially a "no action" plan, typical of those adopted by many of Lincoln's future military leaders. However, Lincoln did learn a thing or two from his aging general. He grasped the importance of holding the Mississippi River, which became part of Lincoln's overall military strategy. He also implemented a blockade of crucial Southern coasts, as Scott had suggested. But the new commander-in-chief was going to be much more aggressive in his campaign to preserve the nation. It was at this point that Lincoln launched his three-year search for a Union general who would do the job for him. He began a quest that all leaders must embark on. He started looking for a chief subordinate who craves responsibility, is a risk-taker, and, most importantly, makes things happen.

In early 1861 Lincoln appointed Gen. Irvin McDowell commanding general of the Army. Even though McDowell formally reported to General Scott, he was the first in a long line of field commanders appointed by and answering directly

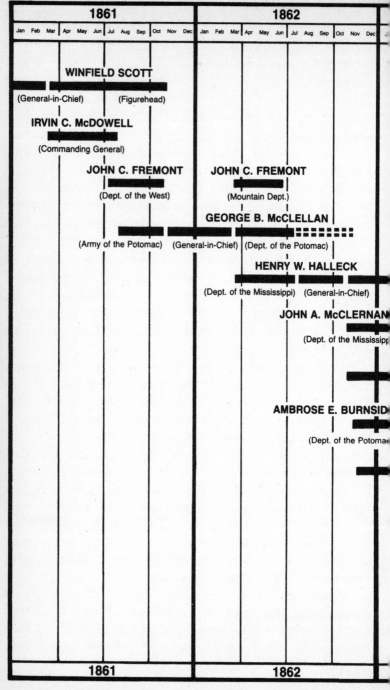

1863	1864	1865
Apr May Jun Jul Aug Sep Oct Nov Dec	Jan Feb Mar Apr May Jun Jul Aug Sep Oct Nov Dec	Jan Feb Mar Apr

HENRY W. HALLECK

(Figurehead)   (Chief of Staff)

WILLIAM S. ROSECRANS

(Dept. of the Cumberland)

NATHANIEL P. BANKS

(Dept. of the Gulf)   (Figurehead)

ULYSSES S. GRANT

(Dept. of the Mississippi)   (Dept. of the West)   (General-in-chief)

JOSEPH HOOKER

(Dept. of the Potomac)

GEORGE G. MEADE

(Dept. of the Potomac)

| 1863 | 1864 | 1865 |

to Lincoln. At this point the president considered Scott a figurehead and consulted with him on an as-needed basis.

McDowell, however, was overwhelmed with the prospect of commanding such a large army and hesitated to take action too quickly. Rather, he elected to build up and train his forces. However, after Fort Sumter the president directed McDowell, through General Scott, to engage the enemy at Manassas, Virginia. It was Lincoln who planned and directed the first major offensive of the Civil War at Bull Run. When McDowell complained and argued for more time to prepare he found the president firm and unwavering: "You are green, it is true," Lincoln told him, "but they are green, also; you are all green alike. . . ."

By the end of July 1861, it had become clear to Lincoln that McDowell was in over his head and that General Scott would soon have to retire. Lincoln needed someone who could build, organize, and train an army, and then formulate and implement a military strategy to invade the South. After four months of command, McDowell demonstrated that he was not going to get the job done. Lincoln decided it was time to try the flamboyant George B. McClellan.

Lincoln appointed McClellan commander of the Army of the Potomac in July 1861 and, three months later, upon the retirement of Scott, general-in-chief. McClellan was a man of impeccable credentials and reputation, and he was an excellent organizer. In truth, Lincoln could not have chosen a better man for the job of staffing, training, and administering the disorganized and defeated troops from the battle of Bull Run. In the long term, however, McClellan's negative side overshadowed any good qualities. Often he overanalyzed and remained inactive. He simply would not fight.

Nearly three months had passed since McClellan's appointment as general-in-chief when, on January 27, 1863, President Lincoln attempted to spur McClellan into action by issuing General War Order #1, which stated that February 22 was to be a day for "a general movement of the Land and Naval forces of the United States against the insurgent forces." As John Hay noted in his diary, Lincoln "wrote it without any consultation and read it to the Cabinet, not for their sanction, but for their information." Lincoln was taking charge and implementing a relatively new method. His chief purpose was to get the war effort off dead center.

But his war order had virtually no effect, and, by early March 1862, General McClellan had still not made any progress in engaging the enemy. Finally, Lincoln's own mounting frustration, coupled with increasing pressure from Congress and his cabinet, forced him to take more decisive action to cure the situation. On March 11, four and a half months after he had appointed McClellan general-in-chief, Lincoln removed much of the general's authority, leaving him with only the Army of the Potomac. At the same time, he created two new departments: The Department of the Mississippi went to Gen. Henry W. Halleck, and the Mountain Department to Gen. John. C. Fremont. This was a radical change in the organization of the military. Again, Lincoln made the decision himself, informed his subordinates, and instituted the new procedure.

By removing some of McClellan's responsibility, Lincoln hoped that the general would somehow be able to devote more time to pursuing the enemy in the field. The president's hopes were dashed, however, as McClellan continued to delay while calling for more troops to beef up his army against what he feared was a force that vastly outnumbered his own. On April 9, 1862, Lincoln wrote a letter to the general urging him to move: "And, once more, let me tell you, it is indispensable to *you* that you strike a blow," pleaded the president. "*I am powerless to help in this. . . .*" In closing, Lincoln stated: "I beg to assure you that I have never written you, or spoken to you, in greater kindness of feeling than now, nor with a fuller purpose to sustain you, so far as in my most anxious judgment, I consistently can. *But you must act.*"

Lincoln was still offering McClellan moral and strategic

support. At the same time, however, he made it clear that any further delays would not be tolerated.

In early May, after another month of inactivity by the Army, Lincoln, accompanied by secretaries Stanton and Chase, traveled to Fort Monroe to initiate action. When McClellan declined to join them because, as he said, he was too busy at the front, Lincoln decided to take charge, immediately directing an assault on Norfolk, Virginia. He ordered the army to bombard the Confederate batteries at Sewall's Point and then proceeded to the Virginia coast where, after actually walking ashore, he determined a satisfactory place for an amphibious landing of troops. Lincoln then returned to the Fort and ordered the attack, which resulted in the Union capture of the city. Chase later recalled that, in his opinion, Norfolk would not have been taken had the president not been right there. And Lincoln had made good on his remark to his friend Orville Browning back in January when he said: "I am thinking of taking the field myself."

Once again, here is a Lincoln principle that modern leaders should not ignore. If your chief subordinates do not move and get the job going, then you should act, decisively and without hesitation. Issue formal "war orders" or, better yet, go to the field and take charge yourself. Set the tone and give your people a message. If your followers see you leading the fight, just as Lincoln took Norfolk, there will be no mistaking what you want them to do.

However, this did not seem to affect McClellan, who did not change his ways. Even though he was supportive, Lincoln knew he must make a change in generals if anything was to be done. After conferring with Winfield Scott at West Point, Lincoln appointed Henry Halleck as general-in-chief on July 11, 1862, exactly four months since he'd split McClellan's command into three departments. McClellan, along with all other generals, would now report to Halleck, a man he'd once commanded. Once again Lincoln tried a different approach in an effort to shake things up and get something going. When he appointed Henry Halleck, he had every intention, at first, of letting him run the whole show. He even authorized Halleck to remove McClellan if he deemed it necessary.

Much to the president's dismay, Halleck did not relieve McClellan who, even though he had been demoted again, would still not fight. In mid-September 1862, Robert E. Lee had ventured into Northern territory only to be met by McClellan's large army. Outnumbered by almost two to one, Lee valiantly outmaneuvered McClellan again and again, inflicting heavy losses on the Union army. But sheer numbers forced him to retreat across the Potomac River. McClellan, feeling that he had won a great victory, wired a message to Washington that his victory was "complete." Lincoln, however, soon discovered that McClellan had no intention of pursuing Lee's battered army into Virginia and that, to the general, "complete victory" meant only that he had defended his ground.

Two weeks after the battle, the president visited McClellan at Antietam in an attempt to light a fire under him. Lincoln lectured McClellan against the dangers of overcautiousness, at the same time telling him that he "felt kindly toward him personally." Lincoln endeavored to get McClellan to take the offensive, but the general replied only that he would move as soon as he felt ready. The president, obviously frustrated by his general's attitude, openly referred to the Army of the Potomac as "McClellan's bodyguard." A month after the battle, when McClellan attempted to stall for time by complaining that his horses were worn out, Lincoln fired off a sarcastic reply that read: "I have just read your dispatch about sore tongued and fatigued horses. Will you pardon me for asking what the horses of your army have done since the battle of Antietam that fatigue anything?"

McClellan, as Lincoln termed it, had "the slows," and was now traveling on the same path as had General Scott; the same path on which Halleck would soon follow. Like Scott, McClellan was being eased out of power. First he lost full

command of the Army (when Lincoln made him only commander of the Army of the Potomac) and then he was forced
to report to Halleck. Eventually, like Scott, he would be out
altogether.

This recurring pattern in Lincoln's treatment of his generals
is interesting because it is a familiar tactic used in many
organizations today. When a subordinate is not performing
adequately, rather than firing the person outright, some
responsibility and authority are removed in the hope that the
individual will be able to perform better with fewer responsibilities. Fairness and human dignity are preserved when this
first step is employed; it gives the unsatisfactory performer a
chance to "turn it around." If behavior and performance are
not reversed, the next step is to get the individual out of the
decision-making process as much as possible. Having the
person report to another superior is a good way to do it. In
McClellan's case, he reported to Halleck. In Scott and Halleck's cases, they became figureheads; all decisions were made
by Lincoln and passed through them to preserve protocol.
Eventually, all three generals were removed from command.
Yet, they were eased out in phases, and each phase gave them
an opportunity to perform well and regain their prior stature.
This process had two advantages for an outstanding leader like
Lincoln. First, it allowed him to get and keep things moving;
and second, it allowed him to preserve the dignity of the
individual as much as possible.

When Lincoln first appointed Henry Halleck as general-in-
chief, he thought him well-qualified and a good selection.
Halleck was, after all, a graduate of West Point, a professional
soldier who studied war tactics and maneuvers. He had
written a book entitled *Elements of Military Art and Science*,
which Lincoln read in early 1862. Even his nickname, "Old
Brains," tended to make one think he was suited to his new
position. Halleck, however, turned out to be no better than
any of his predecessors. After Gen. John Pope's resounding defeat at Second Bull Run, Halleck had recoiled badly,

blaming himself for the loss and refusing to act thereafter. Lincoln observed that he "broke down—nerve and pluck all gone—and has ever since evaded all possible responsibility—little more since that than a first-rate clerk." Halleck's loss of composure came less than two months after his appointment as general-in-chief. But Lincoln would give him time to recover to show what he could do. Halleck, too, would get his three-to-five-month grace period.

Many contemporary corporate executives also give their new chief supervisors a grace period. It's usually called a "honeymoon" and lasts about six months, in which the new manager gets to do just about anything, within reason. Furthermore, the top executive will generally advise his new leader to simply listen for the first three months or so and then make changes. This allows the new leader to truly understand his new position. Lincoln, however, did not have the time to allow his generals a six-month honeymoon. The price to pay for inaction was simply too high, and his philosophy was to give each general only three to five months to show positive results.

When Halleck didn't recover after that period of time, Lincoln took charge. Three and a half months after Halleck's promotion, Lincoln caused another major shake-up of the military. On October 21, 1862, he appointed John A. McClernand to head up the Department of the Mississippi. On October 23, he appointed William S. Rosecrans as head of the Department of the Cumberland. On November 5, he relieved McClellan and appointed Gen. Ambrose E. Burnside to head the Army of the Potomac. And on November 9, he appointed Nathaniel P. Banks leader of the Department of the Gulf. All of this occurred within a three-week period largely because Lincoln was frustrated with Halleck. Although "Old Brains" would retain his impressive title, he would now be only a figurehead, much like Winfield Scott had been. Lincoln had once again taken the bull by the horns. All commanding generals would get their orders from him, sometimes relayed through Halleck. Now, with this lineup, Lincoln would see if there was a real general among them. Lincoln was obviously not afraid to shake things up in an effort to make something positive happen. He would make mistakes, as all leaders do, but the alternative of never winning was unacceptable.

But Lincoln was to be disappointed once more. In fact, he made a serious mistake in his appointment of John A. McClernand on the Mississippi. McClernand had been an Illinois Democrat originally commissioned by the president for political reasons. Even though he was aggressive, he turned out to be a very poor general who was overly ambitious. He was also territorial, wanting all credit for himself. In addition, he wrote long, critical letters to Lincoln complaining about his colleagues, especially Sherman and Grant. His mounting of an aggressive smear campaign against Grant backfired when, on January 25, 1863, three months after his promotion, Lincoln made McClernand report directly to Grant, who now headed all forces along the Mississippi.

Lincoln liked Ulysses S. Grant, who had been looming on the horizon since early 1862, when he had won impressive victories in Tennessee. He'd earned the nickname "Unconditional Surrender" Grant after the capture of Fort Donelson on February 16, the same day that Lincoln promoted him to major general. Casualties had been high in Grant's victories in Tennessee, and there were rumors that he had been drunk during parts of the battles. Many people were calling for Lincoln to dismiss Grant, but the president stood by him. "I can't spare this man," said Lincoln. "He fights!"

Lincoln did not have much luck with generals Nathaniel Banks and William Rosecrans. Both were mediocre leaders who tended to take action only when prodded by the president; Banks, particularly, started out on a sour note with the president. In early November he had promised Lincoln that he would be en route to Louisiana within a week but had then turned around and asked for more supplies and men. On

November 22, the president wrote a biting reprimand to Banks:

> My dear General, this expanding, and piling up on *impedimenta*, has been, so far, almost our ruin, and will be our final ruin if it is not abandoned. . . . You must get back to something like the plan you had then, or your expedition is a failure before you start. You must be off before Congress meets.

Although Banks had won an impressive victory at Port Hudson, Mississippi, with the help of Grant, he turned out to be a relatively weak commanding general. Lincoln eventually sent him off to an administrative job overseeing the reconstruction of Louisiana.

Rosecrans turned out to be just like Banks. He remained in Nashville for the first two months after his appointment to head the armies of the Cumberland, piling up "impedimenta," as Lincoln termed it. In January 1863, he finally engaged the enemy and repulsed a rebel attack at Murfreesboro, Tennessee, forcing them to retreat to Chattanooga. But in his infinite caution and delay, it was another eight months before Rosecrans finally pushed the Confederates out of Chattanooga, and this only after Lincoln forced him into action. Then, in his pursuit of the rebels, Rosecrans was soundly defeated at Chickamauga Creek on September 20, 1863. After this the general lost all ability to lead his men and his own self-control as well. Lincoln described him as "confused and stunned like a duck hit on the head."

A few weeks later, on October 16, President Lincoln gave Ulysses S. Grant command of all the armies in the West. When he received word of his promotion, Grant immediately rode to Chattanooga, relieved Rosecrans, and fortified the city. Lincoln was pleased with the aggressiveness displayed by his new commanding general. Just as he had taken Vicksburg that summer, Grant, in about a month, would win impressive battles at Missionary Ridge and Lookout Mountain, Tennessee. The president seemed to have found the fighting general he had been looking for.

However, Lincoln still had major problems in the East. Ambrose E. Burnside lasted only two and a half months as a replacement for George McClellan as commander of the Army of the Potomac. While Burnside had the reputation of being a fighting general, Lincoln found out very quickly that he was not competent enough to command such a large army. Burnside, who'd accepted the command hesitantly, even admitted as much. A few weeks after the appointment, Lincoln visited Burnside and his troops at Acquia Creek, where he proposed a plan (rejected by both Burnside and Halleck) for attacking Fredericksburg. The president's persistence forced Burnside into an engagement with Robert E. Lee at Fredericksburg, where the commander made several fatal errors in judgment that resulted in a disastrous loss for the Union. Burnside could not accept that there were more than 12,000 casualties as a result of the battle, and he too, like Rosecrans, broke down and lost all control. In the following weeks, the morale of the army began to suffer and when his own subordinates began to openly question his ability, Burnside went to the president to demand their dismissal. Instead Lincoln decided to relieve *Burnside* and replace him with one of those complaining officers, Joe Hooker, on January 25, 1863.

Hooker could manage only five months as the fourth commander of the Army of the Potomac. Here was another general with a nickname that implied action, but "Fighting Joe" turned out to be no better than the rest. Taking over as he did in the winter months, he had the perfect excuse for inactivity—inclement weather. "The Army of the Potomac is stuck in the mud," wrote Lincoln's secretary John Nicolay, "as it has been during nearly the whole of its existence."

When the warm spring weather returned, Lincoln assembled a large party, including his wife and son, to visit General Hooker at Falmouth, Virginia. He wanted to see what the

Army was doing; in addition, he wanted to leave no doubts in Hooker's mind that he was expected to move. Lincoln remained in the field for five days (April 4–10, 1863) living in a tent with his family, mingling with the troops, viewing the Fredericksburg battlefield, and developing strategies with his new commanding general. The president couldn't help but be impressed with the Army of the Potomac, which was now more than 130,000 men strong and, thanks to McClellan, well-drilled and well-equipped. Hooker was confident, and he told Lincoln emphatically that he would take Richmond handily. But the president had heard that before. "The most depressing thing about Hooker," said Lincoln, "is that he is overconfident."

Lincoln returned to Washington somewhat cheered but still skeptical of the army's ability to mount an assault. His reservations were realized in less than a month when Hooker was thoroughly beaten by Robert E. Lee's army at Chancellorsville, Virginia. Hooker had taken a hasty retreat, and Lincoln wanted to know why. On May 7, 1863, he again visited Hooker's camp near Chancellorsville and conferred with the general and his subordinates. Lincoln offered support and direction. He conversed with, and then (as was his habit with Hooker) gave the general a letter that asked if he had in his "mind a plan wholly, or partially formed? If you have," said Lincoln, "prosecute it without interference from me. If you have not, please inform me, so that I, incompetent as I may be, can try [to] assist in the formation of some plan for the Army."

Hooker responded to Lincoln that he had a generalized plan to cross the Rappahannock and engage the enemy even though the Confederates had gained strength through reinforcements. Back in Washington, however, Lincoln heard that Hooker's subordinate officers were openly complaining about their general, as had happened to Burnside. In an effort to resolve the problems, the president summoned his general to the White House to discuss the matter face to face. In his customary letter, Lincoln stated: "I must tell you I have some painful intimations that some of your corps and Division Commanders are not giving you their entire confidence. This would be ruinous, if true; and you should therefore, first of all, ascertain the real facts beyond all possibility of doubt."

When Hooker asked who it was that had been complaining about his abilities, Lincoln refused to divulge the names. Hooker left the president and returned to his army concerned about what had happened. However, his future actions did not change: "Fighting Joe" behaved a great deal like "Old Brains" and "Young Napoleon."

Many corporate executives are faced with the same problem Lincoln encountered. Just as subordinate officers complained about Burnside and Hooker, employees will often gripe about their supervisors. In dealing with this dilemma, modern leaders should take their cue from Lincoln. If your chief executive's subordinates complain, let the executive know about the complaints. This is only fair. He may not know that people are disenchanted, and it will give him time to correct the problem. However, Lincoln would also be the first to say that if you determine that the complaints are true, and nothing changes, it's appropriate to remove the supervisor, especially if he's not doing his job properly.

Only two weeks after a failed attempt to visit Hooker in the field a third time, on June 28, 1863, Lincoln announced to his cabinet that he'd relieved Hooker and replaced him with George Meade (who was formally on Hooker's staff and one of his chief antagonists). Lincoln told the cabinet members that he had "observed in Hooker the same failings that were witnessed in McClellan after the Battle of Antietam,—a want of alacrity to obey, and a greedy call for more troops which could not, and ought not to be taken from other points." And so it went with Hooker, who had now gone the way of his predecessor, Burnside, replaced by one of his own complaining subordinates.

Lincoln and Stanton jointly chose General Meade to succeed Hooker. They needed someone who knew the Army of the Potomac because the troops would have to move quickly. Word had just been received that Robert E. Lee and his Army of Northern Virginia had invaded southern Pennsylvania. When told by Stanton that Meade was from Pennsylvania, where the next crucial battle needed to be fought, Lincoln replied that his new commander would "fight well on his own dunghill."

General Meade immediately mobilized the Army of the Potomac and headed north, keeping himself between Lee's army and Washington. He caught Lee at Gettysburg as both armies were converging on the small town at the same time. Meade bravely dug in and skillfully directed his troops for the three days of battle (July 1–3). On July 5, after a day of inactivity, Robert E. Lee retreated to Virginia. The battle of Gettysburg was a decisive Union victory and Meade was, for the moment, a hero. Meanwhile, in Washington, an elated President Lincoln realized that the war could come to an end immediately if Meade would mount an offensive and crush the severely wounded army of Robert E. Lee. But inexplicably, and much to the chagrin of Lincoln, Meade did not follow through. The commanding general seemed to be satisfied with the victory at Gettysburg and basically only followed Lee south to the Potomac River. In fact, he ordered his troops to "drive from our soil every vestige of the presence of the invader." When Lincoln read this in the Telegraph Office he was shocked. "Drive the invader from our soil!" He cried. "My God! Is that all?" "This is a dreadful reminiscence of McClellan," Lincoln told John Hay. "The same spirit that moved McClellan to claim a great victory because Pennsylvania and Maryland were safe. The hearts of ten million people sunk within them when McClellan raised that shout last fall [at Antietam]. Will our generals never get that idea out of their heads? The whole country is our soil."

When Lee's troops reached the banks of the river, they found that high water prevented their crossing. They were trapped, and Lincoln knew now that if only Meade would attack the war would be ended. But, again, Meade stalled and deliberated with his officers as to what course of action he should take. In those seven days of cautious hesitation, the Potomac River receded and Lee's army crossed to safety in Virginia. When the president received word of Lee's escape, he was inconsolable and angered. He told Secretary of the Navy Gideon Welles that he had dreaded yet expected what had happened. "And that, my God," said Lincoln, "is the last of the Army of the Potomac! There is bad faith somewhere. Meade has been pressed and urged, but only one of his generals was for an immediate attack, was ready to pounce on Lee; the rest held back. What does it mean, Mr. Welles? Great God! What does it mean?" Lincoln had never been so visibly upset and he vented his anger in a harsh, chiding letter of criticism to Meade.

After cooling down, Lincoln reconsidered and did not send the letter. He realized that Meade had secured a great victory, and the president was grateful for "the service he did at Gettysburg." But Lincoln later told his son, Robert, that if he "had gone up there, I could have whipped them myself." Meade, for his part, was severely stung by the president's dissatisfaction. He never really did anything after the battle of Gettysburg until Ulysses Grant was named the new general-in-chief.

In a meeting with Meade several weeks later, Lincoln explained his view of the general's conduct after the battle of Gettysburg: "I'll be hanged," said Lincoln, "if I could think of anything else than an old woman trying to shoo her geese across a creek."

Contemporary leaders who experience difficulties finding the right chief subordinate can take comfort in the knowledge that at this point in the Civil War, Lincoln had spent more than two and a half years searching for an aggressive general who could do the job. But his persistence had not waned. In fact, after Lee's escape at Gettysburg, his determination may have been rejuvenated.

During the inactive months of the winter of 1863–1864, Lincoln formulated plans for what was to be his last major shake-up of the American military system. On March 10,

1864, Lincoln officially promoted Ulysses S. Grant to the rank of lieutenant general and consolidated all the armies of the United States under him. Only a few weeks earlier, Congress had passed a bill (possibly at Lincoln's request) reestablishing this rank and authorizing the president to appoint any one man to that position. Prior to Grant only two men had ever held the title: George Washington and Winfield Scott. Grant was now the new general-in-chief and for the first time since early 1861 the United States had a single commander. Lincoln had taken one more drastic step, and this time it would work.

In the days surrounding the general's promotion, Lincoln did something that many modern-day corporate executives do—he counseled Grant thoroughly in several private meetings. He wanted his new chief subordinate to get off on the right foot, and to handle himself well in public. A day before the official White House ceremony marking the new move, Lincoln told him that he intended to read a few appropriate remarks and suggested that Grant do the same since he was not used to making speeches. The president further suggested that in his commentary he say something to appease other generals who felt that they should have had the job and, in addition, to compliment the Army of the Potomac. Shortly after the appointment was conferred, Lincoln called Grant aside in private to discuss the ongoing military situation. He told his new commanding general that he could best illustrate the message he was trying to get across by means of a story:

> At one time there was a great war among the animals, and one side had great difficulty in getting a commander who had sufficient confidence in himself. Finally, they found a monkey . . . who said that he thought he could command their army if his tail could be made a little longer. So they got more tail. . . . He looked at it admiringly, and then thought he ought to have a little more still. This was added, and again he called for more. The splicing process was repeated

> many times, until they had coiled [the monkey's] tail around the room, filling all the space. [Then] they wrapped it around his shoulders . . . until its weight broke him down.

After hearing this story from Lincoln, Grant reassured the president that he would not call for any more troops than were absolutely necessary.

In implementing the new major military shake-up, Lincoln also made Gen. Henry Halleck the nation's first chief of staff. The position suited "Old Brains"; all he had to do was act as liaison between Lincoln and Grant. It was a perfect arrangement because Grant insisted on having his office in the field, which Lincoln preferred. Grant traveled with the Army of the Potomac, an arrangement that also worked well for Meade, who was better suited to taking orders than giving them. Grant would ride back to Washington regularly to confer and discuss strategy with the president; together they worked out the offensive movements on all fronts that were to eventually end the war. At one work session, Grant unveiled to the president his grand plan to involve all the armies of the Union in a centralized attack against the South, prompting Lincoln to cheerfully comment that "those not skinning can hold a leg." Lincoln found that he could effectively give Grant a free hand to run the war effort. He didn't have to spend an inordinate amount of time overseeing this general the way he had with McClellan and the others. Yet Lincoln never really relinquished total control and authority. He was still the president, and even with General Grant he would persist in monitoring military operations, exerting his personal influence when he felt it necessary.

On May 3, 1864, less than two months after he had assumed full command, Grant hurled his massive army full force at Robert E. Lee in the bloody conflict known as the Wilderness Campaign. Lincoln waited anxiously in Washington as the battle raged on but heard nothing from Grant for five days. During the interim, when asked if he'd heard anything from the field, Lincoln is reported to have quipped: "Grant has gone into the Wilderness, crawled in, drawn up the ladder, and pulled in the hole after him, and I guess we'll have to wait till he comes out before we know just what he's up to." Grant finally communicated that he had pushed through the wilderness but, in so doing, had suffered enormous casualties. He was forcing Lee to retreat by attacking him again and again but was not winning any major victories. "I propose to fight it out on this line if it takes all summer," vowed Grant. This was music to Lincoln's ears. Never before had he had a general who was so aggressive. "It is the dogged pertinacity of Grant that wins," the president told John Hay. Grant, too, admired Lincoln's tenacity. After he received a telegram from the president exhorting him to "hold on with a bulldog grip, and chew and choke as much as possible," Grant laughed and remarked that "the President has more nerve than any of his advisors."

Following major setbacks at Spotsylvania and Cold Harbor, on June 18, Grant settled in for a siege at Petersburg, Virginia. Lee had dug in and could not be penetrated without major loss of life. This disheartened Lincoln, and he decided to go to the field to assess the situation. From June 20 to June 23 he was at Grant's field headquarters at City Point, where he met with the troops, telling stories and anecdotes, and conferring seriously with Grant on the situation at hand. This was the same tack he used with all the generals before Grant, further proof that he treated them all equally in the beginning. Lincoln's roving leadership style was ubiquitous.

At this meeting, Grant reassured the president that he would get to Lee eventually and that he had nothing to worry about. Impressed with the general's determination, Lincoln commented to one of Grant's staff that once he "gets possession of a place, he holds on to it as if he had inherited it." When the president returned to Washington, Secretary Welles noted that he was in "good spirits." The journey had "done him good, physically, and strengthened him mentally and inspired confidence in the general and his army."

Within a week of his return to the capital, Lincoln was surprised to learn that in order to divert Union troops from Lee's front, Confederate general Jubal Early had mounted an offensive through the Shenandoah Valley and, by mid-July, had made it to the outskirts of Washington, D.C. (Silver Spring, Maryland, to be exact). On July 12, President Lincoln visited Fort Stevens and became one of the few American presidents to come directly under enemy fire. As he stood on the parapet of the fort surveying the situation and watching troop movements, some of Early's men opened fire and a soldier standing near Lincoln was shot.

General Grant quickly reinforced the troops around Washington and pushed the Confederates back into the Shenandoah. Lincoln, however, was concerned that Early had gotten so far so quickly. He called for a field meeting with Grant and on July 31 met with his commanding general at Fortress Monroe. They not only discussed his concern about Early's Washington raid; Lincoln also reminded Grant that it was an election year. If Lincoln was to be reelected in November he needed military successes, and he encouraged Grant to keep that fact in mind as he proceeded with his offensive campaign. The next day, August 1, Grant (possibly directed by Lincoln) ordered Gen. Phil Sheridan to take charge of all the forces in the Washington area, pursue Early into the Shenandoan Valley, and "follow the Confederates to the death." This was the beginning of Sheridan's remarkably successful campaign, which ended at Winchester, Virginia, on October 19 (three weeks before the election), with all of the Shenandoah Valley under Northern control.

General Grant tended to pick men in his own mold to lead his armies in the field. Phil Sheridan fit his style, as did William Tecumseh Sherman, whose Army of the Cumberland cut a swath into Georgia that resulted in the capture of Atlanta on September 2. This news hit Washington just three weeks after Admiral Farragut had captured Mobile Bay in Alabama and, coupled with Sheridan's victory in Virginia, virtually assured Lincoln's reelection. The next six months would see an endless string of Union victories that all but destroyed the Confederacy. The fall of such Southern strongholds as Nashville, Savannah, Wilmington, Columbia, Petersburg, and Richmond insured a final Union victory that was to come at Appomattox Courthouse in Virginia on April 9, 1865.

One cannot help but wonder if Lincoln's July 31 venture to Fortress Monroe to confer with Grant was not the catalyst for the entire chain of events. One thing is certain: It was President Lincoln's courage, stamina, fortitude, and persistence that led the way to the preservation of the nation. He demanded action and promoted the generals who achieved results. "I, who am not a specially brave man," he once said, "have had to sustain the sinking courage of these professional fighters in critical times."

Abraham Lincoln's entire direction of the war effort can be summed up in one short sentence of a telegram he relayed to Grant on April 7, 1865. Sheridan, who was hammering at Lee's army in Virginia, had wired to Grant: "If the thing be pressed I think Lee will surrender." After reading the message, Lincoln swiftly replied: "Let the *thing* be pressed!"

All leaders should realize that they can't do everything on their own. They simply must have people below them who will do what is necessary to insure success. Those subordinates who will take risks, act without waiting for direction, and ask for responsibility rather than reject it, should be treated as your most prized possessions. Such individuals are exceedingly rare and worth their weight in gold. And when you finally find one—as Lincoln found Grant—they tend to multiply. The "Grants" of the world will choose others in their own image, just as Lincoln's Grant chose such aggressive generals as Sheridan and Sherman rather than procrastinators like McClellan and Hooker.

Corporate executives can possess great vision and be able to provide all the direction in the world, just as Lincoln did. But they can't succeed without a man like U. S. Grant to carry out the company's mission.

LINCOLN PRINCIPLES

★ Choose as your chief subordinates those people who crave responsibility and take risks.

★ Go out into the field with your leaders, and stand or fall with the battle.

★ If employees gripe about one of your chief supervisors, and the complaints are true, do not be afraid to remove him.

★ Give your followers all the support you can, and act on the presumption that they will do the best they can with what you give them.

★ Provide your managers a three-to-five-month grace period to see if they will take action and perform adequately.

★ If they don't perform adequately, ease them out of power gradually, always giving them ample time to turn it around.

★ Beware of subordinates who keep piling up information without ever really accomplishing anything.

★ Coach and counsel a new executive so that he or she may get off on the right foot. Remember, you *want* him to succeed.

★ Do not forget that aggressive leaders tend to choose employees in their own image.

★ Let the *thing* be pressed.

Still the question recurs "can we do better?" The dogmas of the quiet past are inadequate to the stormy present. The occasion is piled high with difficulty, and we must rise with the occasion. As our case is new, so *we must think anew, and act anew*.

> Lincoln, in his Annual Message to Congress, exhorting its members to join him in a united venture to be conducted by the executive and legislative branches of government (December 1, 1862)

12 / *Encourage Innovation*

Genuine leaders, such as Abraham Lincoln, are not only instruments *of* change, they are catalysts *for* change. Lincoln understood early in his presidency that he'd have to virtually rebuild and reorganize the government and its armed forces. The nation was obviously not prepared for such a formidable threat as armed insurrection. Change was imminent. A transformation needed to take place—immediately.

Lincoln effected the change needed by being extraordinarily decisive and by creating an atmosphere of entrepreneurship that fostered innovative techniques. In so doing, he not only got things moving, he also gained commitment from a wide array of individuals who were excited at the prospect of seeing their ideas implemented. He adopted a "more than one way to skin a cat" attitude and would not be consumed with methodology.

Lincoln's obsessive quest for results tended to create a

climate for risk taking and innovation. Inevitably there were failures, but Lincoln had great tolerance for failure because he knew that if his generals were not making mistakes they were not moving. "Always glad to have your suggestions," he encouraged General Grant in 1864. "I say try," he once advised Gen. George McClellan, "if we never try, we shall never succeed." The president viewed the failures of his generals as mistakes, learning events, or steps in the right direction. Rarely did Lincoln assail his subordinates for a loss in battle. Rather, he tended to stand by his commanders, offering them support and giving them encouragement. After the first battle of Bull Run, Lincoln visited Gen. Irvin McDowell and told him: "I have not lost a particle of confidence in you." He did the same thing with Burnside after Fredericksburg, Hooker after Chancellorsville, and Grant when he stalled at Petersburg after the Wilderness Campaign. In each case Lincoln visited his defeated general in the field and offered his full support. The last thing that Lincoln wanted was a brooding or depressed leader (like Halleck or Rosecrans) who had lost his nerve and could fight no more.

Lincoln essentially treated his subordinates as equals; they were colleagues in a joint effort. He had enough confidence in himself that he was not threatened by skillful generals or able cabinet officials. Rather than surround himself with "yes" men, he associated with people who really knew their business, people from whom he could learn something, whether they were antagonistic or not. An often overlooked component of leadership is this ability to learn from people and experiences, from successes and failures. The best leaders never stop learning. They possess a special capacity to be taught by those with whom they come into contact. In essence, this ongoing accumulation of knowledge prepares the organization for change.

Abraham Lincoln was naturally inquisitive, and he possessed this inherent capacity to learn. He also had the desire to learn new things, which led him to be unusually innovative. It is no wonder that he changed the American presidency so profoundly in the span of only four years. He also expected and encouraged the same creative and resourceful behavior from his subordinates. The more contemporary thinking of Tom Peters fits right in with Lincoln's leadership philosophy. Peters, in *Thriving on Chaos*, advocates turning everyone into an innovator by "supporting committed champions, modeling innovation, and supporting past failures."

One of Lincoln's favorite stories, one he told often, was designed to encourage people to innovate, to take action on their own initiative, without waiting for orders:

> It seems that there was this colonel, who when raising his regiment in Missouri, proposed to his men that he should do all the swearing for the regiment. They assented; and for months no instance was known of violation of the promise. The colonel had a teamster named John Todd, who, as roads were not always the best, had some difficulty in commanding his temper and tongue. John happened to be driving a mule team through a series of mudholes a little worse than usual, when he burst forth into a volley of profanity.
>
> The colonel took notice of the offense and brought John to account. "John," said he, "didn't you promise to let me do all the swearing for the regiment?" "Yes, I did, Colonel," he replied, "but the fact was the swearing had to be done then or not at all, and you weren't there to do it."

Years before assuming the presidency, Lincoln had shown his interest in innovation when, on March 10, 1849 (at age forty), he received a patent for a new method of making grounded boats more buoyant. (He is the only United States president to have secured a patent.) Thereafter, he tried to stay up to date on modern scientific breakthroughs. Many years after his patent had been issued, he revealed his great respect and passion for innovation when he stated that "the nation's patent system . . . secured to the inventor, for a limited time, the exclusive use of his invention; and thereby added the fuel of *interest* to the *fire* of genius, in the discovery and production of new and useful things."

After he became president and moved to Washington, Lincoln must have been surprised to find that his interest in new ideas would be tantalized over and over again. Numerous businessmen and inventors visited the Executive Mansion, taking advantage of the new president's "open" office hours. In addition, hundreds of letters poured in requesting that the government purchase a particular invention that would shorten the war. Another man in his position might have ignored or even scoffed at such proposals, but not Lincoln. Not only did he review every request; he set up dozens of demonstrations in and around Washington that he personally attended. By doing so, he was acting as something of a one-man research and development department. These demonstrations, mostly of weapons, were not only fun for Lincoln; they were an important part of his overall strategy to enhance the tools of war through the evolution of modern technology. He was astute enough to understand the importance of gaining new and effective weapons as soon as was humanly possible.

Lincoln observed the ascension of hot-air reconnaissance balloons and the throwing of pontoon bridges across the Potomac River. He opened the way for the ironclad ship, the *Monitor*, to be built. Once he miraculously escaped injury while witnessing the trial test of a Hyde rocket that exploded prematurely. He also screened new types of bullets, flame throwers, gunpowder, and other ammunition. The president even brought one inventor into a regular meeting of his cabinet to demonstrate a new breech-loading cannon.

Perhaps Lincoln's greatest contribution in this area was his screening and support for the new breech-loading rifles that were, at the end of 1861, just becoming dependable. On

October 15, he directed the chief of ordnance, Gen. J. W. Ripley, to order 25,000 Marsh breechloaders. But Ripley had decreed early in the war (because he believed it would be of short duration) that he would not waste his department's time with processing any new proposed weapons, so he did not follow through on the president's order. However, on December 26, Lincoln ordered Ripley to purchase 10,000 Spenser repeating rifles, and this time the president had his way. Lincoln had personally fired both rifles and was convinced that they would make an enormous difference in the war.

Lincoln made himself aware of any and all new technological advances so they could be implemented first by the Union, well before the Confederacy had time to act. He was quick and decisive in employing these new advances and made every attempt to get new weapons into his soldier's hands immediately, often overcoming government red tape and bureaucracy that might have delayed their use in combat. Overall, Lincoln's philosophy and handling of the most up-to-date technology available at the time was brilliant. Moreover, it has amazing parallels with the 1980s movement in business and industry labeled "High Tech."

A leader's ability to develop innovative ideas and ask for people's help in implementing them may seem to be obvious keys to success. But the sad fact is that too many of today's leaders resign themselves to the limits imposed on them by flawed systems rather than rethinking those systems. This seems especially true in America as opposed to Japan, where innovation is a way of life.

Rather than inhibiting progress or sapping energy, innovative thinking actually increases an organization's chances of survival. With today's technology changing so rapidly, modern corporations simply must be able to respond and innovate. This is particularly true of the computer industry, for example, where today's greatest, most advanced invention is often tomorrow's dinosaur.

Lincoln showed that everyone, from foot soldier to president, can contribute to the nation's success. And even during his most difficult times, Lincoln continued to call on his subordinates to screen new advances, implement ideas, and win while learning. He realized that, as an executive leader, it was his chief responsibility to create the climate of risk-free entrepreneurship necessary to foster effective innovation.

LINCOLN PRINCIPLES

- ★ When the occasion is piled high with difficulty, rise with it. Think anew and act anew.
- ★ Don't lose confidence in your people when they fail.
- ★ Let your subordinates know that you are always glad to have their suggestions.
- ★ If you never try, you'll never succeed.
- ★ Except in matters of broad policy, encourage subordinates to take action on their own initiative, without waiting for orders.
- ★ Remember that the best leaders never stop learning.
- ★ Surround yourself with people who really know their business, and avoid "yes" men.
- ★ Be quick and decisive at employing new advances and make every attempt at getting new weapons into your soldiers' hands immediately.

PART IV
COMMUNICATION

Extemporaneous speaking should be practiced and cultivated. It is the lawyer's avenue to the public. However able and faithful he may be in other respects, people are slow to bring him business if he cannot make a speech.

> From Lincoln's notes for a law lecture intended to advise younger lawyers how best to succeed (July 1, 1850)

13 / *Master the Art of Public Speaking*

In the decade of the 1980s Ronald Reagan was labeled the Great Communicator. But as someone who was able to persuade through rhetoric, Reagan is virtually dwarfed by Lincoln. It's well known that Lincoln wrote his own speeches, many of which are today regarded as masterpieces of poetic and artistic expression. He was an eloquent public speaker who had the capacity to raise the emotions of his audience. Also, he was one of the best extemporaneous speakers this nation has ever known, as attested to in the transcripts of the Lincoln–Douglas debates. He penned the Emancipation Proclamation and wrote thousands of letters and notes to anyone with whom he felt he needed to communicate. The sheer volume of his collected works (which amounts to more words than are in the Bible) is testament to his commitment to effective communication.

Even in his youth, well before he became president, Lincoln's impressive oratorical and communicative skills were well known. When Stephen A. Douglas heard that he would be running against Abraham Lincoln for the United States Senate in 1858, he knew that he was up against a formidable opponent. Douglas called him "the strong man of his party—full of wit, facts, dates, and the best stump-speaker with droll-ways and dry jokes in the west. He is as honest as he is shrewd, and if I beat him my victory will be hardly won."

In the six years before his presidency, Lincoln greatly expanded his reputation not only as a spokesman for the common man but also a powerful public speaker. During those years (1854–1860) he dramatically increased his popularity with the citizens of his native Illinois by making more than 175 speeches, many of them extemporaneous. Lincoln realized the value of being able to communicate in such a manner, and public speaking was part of his overall strategy to make himself more well known. In 1850, he wrote: "Extemporaneous speaking should be practiced and cultivated. It is the lawyer's avenue to the public. However able and faithful he may be in other respects, people are slow to bring him business if he cannot make a speech." In making so many speeches, Lincoln perfected his ability to persuade and influence people, a skill that would come in handy after he became president. To witness one of Lincoln's speeches was apparently quite an experience. He had a high-pitched, treble voice that tended to become even more shrill when he became excited. At times, it was even unpleasant. But his voice was a great asset because it could be heard at the farthest reaches of the crowds that gathered outdoors to hear him speak. At times, he also used considerable body language when he spoke. To emphasize a point, for example, Lincoln would "bend his knees, crouch, and then spring up vehemently to his toes."

As a successful lawyer in Illinois, Lincoln was also well known for his extraordinary courtroom abilities. He pleaded more cases in front of the State Supreme Court than any lawyer had prior to him, or has since. His timing and intuitive sensing of the mood of a jury was unparalleled. Lincoln was also bright and had an alert and lucid mind that made him quick on his feet. He could recall facts and figures on a moment's notice and was also capable of using appropriate anecdotes and humorous stories.

It's important to note that Lincoln prepared himself thoroughly for his public speaking engagements. Often he would write out every word of his address and then read from the text during the presentation. He spent hours, sometimes days and weeks, researching his subject and, as one contemporary observed, "he never considered anything he had written to be finished until published, or if a speech, until he delivered it." Lincoln's most famous speeches were exhaustively researched, analyzed, and practiced; frequently they were printed and handed out to reporters before he presented them. This was the case for Lincoln's renowned "House Divided" speech given at the Republican state convention at Springfield in 1858. Nicolay and Hay called it "the most carefully prepared speech of his whole life. Every word of it was written, every sentence had been tested. . . ."

Lincoln's preparation paid off because most Republicans hailed it as an eloquent presentation of the party's platform. The speech appeared in papers across Illinois, and Horace Greeley even printed it in the *New York Tribune* under the heading "Republican Principles."

On February 27, 1860, in New York City, Lincoln gave what was perhaps the most important speech of his political career—the Cooper Institute address. This was his first venture back East, where he was viewed largely as an uncouth westerner. With just a few months remaining until the Republican National Convention would select a presidential candidate, Lincoln realized that the stakes were extraordinarily high. After accepting the invitation to speak in October, he worked on his address on and off for more than three months, carefully researching his facts and choosing his wording. On the night he was to speak, a crowd of about 1,500 people paid twenty-five cents each and jammed into the Cooper Institute. All were curious about this frontier man they had heard so much about. As he approached the podium, one reporter felt sorry for him:

> When Lincoln rose to speak, I was greatly disappointed. He was tall, tall, oh, so tall, and so angular and awkward that I had for an instant a feeling of pity for so ungainly a man . . . His clothes were black and ill-fitting, badly wrinkled—as if they had been jammed carelessly into a small trunk. His bushy head, with the stiff black hair thrown back, was balanced on a long and lean head-stalk, and when he raised his hands in an opening gesture, I noticed that they were very large. He began in a low tone of voice—as if he were used to speaking out-doors and was afraid of speaking too loud.
>
> He said, "Mr. Cheerman," instead of "Mr. Chairman," and employed many other words with an old-fashioned pronunciation. I said to myself, "Old fellow, you won't do; it is all very well for the Wild West, but this will never go down in New York." But pretty soon he began to get into the subject; he straightened up, made regular and graceful gestures; his face lighted as with an inward fire; the whole man was transfigured.
>
> I forgot the clothing, his personal appearance, and his individual peculiarities. Presently, forgetting myself, I was on my feet with the rest, yelling like a wild Indian, cheering the wonderful man. In the closing parts of his argument you could hear the gentle sizzling of the gas burners.

During the speech, Lincoln largely attacked the proslavery views of Stephen A. Douglas, who had asserted that the Founding Fathers had sanctioned the institution of slavery. Through his own exhaustive research, Lincoln proved that twenty-one of the thirty-nine signers of the Constitution of the United States had at one time or another voted to prohibit slavery in the country. Lincoln had proved Douglas wrong, to the delight of the crowd. Later in the address, he cautioned Republicans that "even though much provoked, let us do nothing through passion and ill temper." He concluded with a powerful admonition to hold fast to their beliefs:

> Neither let us be slandered from our duty by false accusations against us, nor frightened from it by menaces of destruction to the Government nor of dungeons to ourselves. LET US HAVE FAITH THAT RIGHT MAKES MIGHT, AND IN THAT FAITH, LET US, TO THE END, DARE TO DO OUR DUTY AS WE UNDERSTAND IT.

The audience cheered and applauded throughout Lincoln's speech, and when he had concluded they gave him a standing ovation while waving hats and handkerchiefs overhead. People also rushed to the podium to shake his hand and congratulate him. The prairie lawyer from Illnois was a smash hit with the eastern Republicans of New York, and soon his speech would be printed in total all across the Northeast. Lincoln's thorough preparation had paid off, and years later he would comment how important that particular speech was and how he felt that he became president largely because of its success.

Even though he thoroughly prepared many of his addresses, it appears that Lincoln possessed a true gift when it came to communicating his feelings and emotions. That talent can be readily observed in one of his shortest and most moving speeches, his farewell remarks to the people of Springfield who'd gathered at the railway station to see him off to Washington. At eight o'clock on the morning of February 11, 1861, the president-elect arrived at the depot with his family to find that more than a thousand of his friends, neighbors, and colleagues had gathered to say good-bye. Moved by their presence, and feeling somewhat obligated to say a few words, Lincoln made the following impromptu speech:

> My friends—no one, not in my situation, can appreciate my feeling of sadness at this parting. To this place, and the kindness of these people, I owe everything. Here I have lived a quarter of a century, and have passed from a young to an old man. Here my children have been born, and one is buried. I now leave, not knowing when, or whether ever, I may return, with a task before me greater than that which rested upon Washington. Without the assistance of that Divine Being, who ever attended him, I cannot succeed. With that assistance I cannot fail. Trusting in Him, who can go with me, and remain with you and be everywhere for good, let us confidently hope that all will yet be well. To His care commending you, as I hope in your prayers you will commend me, I bid you an affectionate farewell.

Interestingly enough, after he became president, and especially while he was running for office, Lincoln substantially curtailed his public speaking, particularly extemporaneous remarks. His strategy during the election of 1860 was to remain silent. He was the more moderate, middle-of-the-road candidate, and the Democratic party was effectively split into a Northern and Southern faction. If he did not speak, he reasoned, he would alienate few people and would probably win the election. On June 19, 1860, he wrote to a friend: "In my present position . . . by the lessons of the past, and the united voice of all discreet friends, I am neither [to] write or speak a word for the public." Less than a month later he told a group: "It has been my purpose, since I have been placed in my present position, to make no speeches. . . . Kindly let me be silent."

Lincoln's silence paid off in a stunning victory. Yet when he took office he did not change his philosophy about speaking in public. Like many modern presidents, Lincoln watched what he said for fear of being misinterpreted or, worse yet, misquoted by the press. "In my present position," he said in 1862, "it is hardly proper for me to make speeches. Every word is so closely noted that it will not do to make trivial ones. . . ." In 1864 he stated: "Everything I say, you know, goes into print. If I make a mistake it doesn't merely affect me nor you, but the country. I therefore ought at least try not to make mistakes." President Lincoln's relationship with the press corps of the day, as with most people, was good. He treated reporters the same way he treated everyone else. He respected them, and, when the opportunity presented itself, he would make pleasant conversation and tell some of his jokes. The day he was elected, Lincoln smiled at the newsmen present and quipped: "Well boys, your troubles are over now, mine have just begun."

As president, Lincoln was an intelligent communicator. He was careful about what he said, and he thought before he spoke. Every one of his major addresses while in office (including the First and Second Inaugurals, the Gettysburg Address, and his Last Public Address) was meticulously prepared and read from a completed manuscript. In the case of each there was a specific message Lincoln wanted to convey. He was not talking just to hear his own voice.

Lincoln's practice of writing his speeches before they were delivered gave him the time to think about what he wanted to say and insured that his message would come across the way he intended. He became so dependent on this style and format that, to a large extent, he relied on writing as a chief form of communication. Often he coupled written documents with oral discussions. This procedure was not limited just to formal speeches. For example, Lincoln wrote the substance of his conversations with Joseph Hooker *before* they got together and then, at the conclusion of their meeting, he handed the general a letter to take with him for further contemplation. Lincoln wanted no mistaking what his meaning or directives were in these instances, and there could be no misinterpretation when two senses, sight *and* sound, were appealed to rather than one. Lincoln picked up this technique when he was a lawyer, as was recalled by his law partner William Herndon:

> Mr. Lincoln's habits, methods of reading law, politics, poetry, etc., were to come into the office, pick up a book, newspaper, etc., and to sprawl himself out on the sofa, chair, etc., and read aloud much to my annoyance. I have asked him often why he did so, and his invariable reply was: "I catch the idea by two senses. But when I read aloud I hear what is read and I see it, and hence two senses get it and I remember it better, if I do not understand it better."

In recent years, modern leadership theory has stressed the importance of effective communication. James MacGregor Burns wrote that "the Leader's fundamental act is to induce people to be aware or conscious of what they feel—to feel their true needs so strongly, to define their values so meaningfully, that they can be moved to purposeful action." Lee Iacocca put it more simply by stating: "The only way you can motivate people is to communicate with them." Effective communication also shapes values for people by "not only bringing company philosophy to life . . . ," as Peters and Austin put it, but also "helps newcomers understand how shared values affect individual performance."

But there is more to communication than just motivation and value-shaping. "Leaders," wrote Warren Bennis and Burt Nanus, "articulate and define what has previously remained implicit or unsaid; then they invent images, metaphors, and models that provide a focus for new attention. By so doing they consolidate or challenge prevailing wisdom. In short, an essential factor in leadership is the capacity to influence and organize meaning for members of the organization. . . . Communication creates meaning for people. Or should. It's the only way any group, small or large, can become aligned behind the overarching goals of an organization."

The adage "It's not what you say but how you say it" also applies to Abraham Lincoln's communication style. He combined a well-rounded, albeit self-taught, education with wit and sincerity to serve as the nucleus of the archetypal communicator.

Today's leaders would do well to embody Lincoln's simple, straightforward approach, especially when sending complex messages that can be easily misread. Messages are more often "heard" when the communicator is honest, sincere, and succinct. In other words, say what you mean, and mean what you say.

Lincoln built credibility by being consistent and clear when speaking to others. But he did it with more than words; his actions mirrored what he said. Nothing frustrates subordinates more than receiving mixed messages. No matter what the method of communication—memos, discussions, phone calls, etc.—to lead effectively you must be clear and confident in what you have to say, and then you must follow through.

LINCOLN PRINCIPLES

★ Be your organization's best stump-speaker, with droll ways and dry jokes.

★ Extemporaneous speaking is your avenue to the public.

★ Use a variety of body language when you speak.

★ Prepare yourself thoroughly for your public speaking engagements.

★ Never consider anything you write to be finished until published or, if a speech, until you deliver it.

★ Remember that there will be times when you should simply not speak. Say to your listeners: "Kindly let me be silent."

★ Try not to make mistakes when you speak publicly. Everything you say is intently heard. If you make a mistake it doesn't merely affect you but the organization as well.

★ You should often couple written documents with verbal discussions, thereby catching the idea with two senses rather than just one. Both you and your subordinates will remember it better, even if you do not understand it better.

14 / *Influence People Through Conversation and Storytelling*

Though Abraham Lincoln was an outstanding writer and public speaker, he was even more adept at the art of conversation. He could talk to anyone, brilliant scientist, wily politician, visiting head of state, or simple backwoods farmer. He had a terrific sense of humor and often sprinkled his conversations with witty stories and humorous anecdotes that he used as persuasive tools. He has come to be regarded as the only president of the United States who was a true humorist in the tradition of Mark Twain or Will Rogers.

Conversation was Lincoln's chief form of persuasion and the single most important and effective aspect of his leadership style. One on one, Lincoln could convince anybody of just about anything. He enjoyed talking to people, which was one reason he created such open access to the White House. Everyone and anyone was invited to come in and talk to him. But even the brightest leading citizens of the era were dominated by Lincoln during a personal exchange. Many who called on him at the White House to obtain some favor found themselves in the hall wondering how Lincoln got rid of them. Thurlow Weed, a prominent journalist and political organizer, once sat down after a meeting with him and wrote a letter to Lincoln that stated, in part: "I do not, when with you, say half I intend, partly because I do not like to 'crank,' and partly because you talk me out of my convictions and apprehensions. So bear with me, please, now, till I free my mind." In turn, Lincoln, amusingly, once wrote to Weed: "I am sure if we could meet we would not part with any unpleasant impression on either side."

Carl Schurz, a Republican contemporary of Lincoln, and later a Union general, recounted his first meeting with the future president:

> All at once, after the train had left a way-station, I observed a great commotion among my fellow-passengers, many of whom jumped from their seats and pressed eagerly around a tall man who had just entered the car. They addressed him in the most familiar style: "Hello, Abe! How are you?" and so on. And he responded in the same manner: "Good-evening, Ben! How are you, Joe? Glad to see you, Dick!" and there was much laughter at some things he said, which, in the confusion of voices, I could not understand. "Why," exclaimed my companion, the committee-man, "there's Lincoln, himself!" He pressed through the crowd and introduced me to Abraham Lincoln, whom I then saw for the first time. . . . He received me with an off-hand cordiality, like an old acquaintance . . . and we sat down together. In a somewhat high-pitched but pleasant voice . . . [he] talked in so simple and familiar a strain, and his manner and homely phrase were so absolutely free from any semblance of self-consciousness or pretension of superiority, that I soon felt as if I had known him all my life, and we had very

long been close friends. He interspersed our conversations with all sorts of quaint stories, each of which had
a witty point applicable to the subject in hand, and not
seldom concluded an argument in such a manner that
nothing more was to be said.

Carl Schurz was not the only person who heard Abraham
Lincoln tell a story. As a matter of fact, nearly everyone who
came in contact with our sixteenth president heard him relate
some kind of yarn. Lincoln, it turned out, had an overwhelming inventory of anecdotes, jokes, and stories; furthermore, he
possessed the ability to instantly pull out just the right one for
any situation that might arise. Lincoln was a master at the art
of storytelling, and he used that ability purposefully and
effectively when he was president of the United States.

Storytelling came naturally to Lincoln. He inherited the ability
partly from his father, Thomas Lincoln, who was a popular
yarn-spinner of his day. After a long day's work as a lawyer riding
the circuit in Illinois, Abraham would pass the time with his
colleagues at the local tavern, where each would take turns telling
a favorite anecdote. Often they would hold storytelling contests
in front of standing-room-only crowds eager to be amused and
entertained. Over the years, Lincoln not only built up a good
supply of tales but also perfected his skill at relating them.

Lincoln's humor was a major component of his ability to
persuade people. He knew the effect it had and used it to the
utmost. It also aided him politically by becoming an obsession
with the public. People became fascinated with his quick wit
and hilarious stories; as a result, many of his humorous
anecdotes found their way into print while he was still alive.
Literally hundreds of stories were attributed to Lincoln that
the president himself had never even heard.

During his years in the White House, Lincoln's storytelling became so legendary that amusing tales started to circulate about *him*.
One that he was fond of telling on himself was about two Quaker
women in a railway coach who were overheard in a conversation:

"I think Jefferson will succeed," said the first.

"Why does thee think so?" asked the second.

"Because Jefferson is a praying man."

"And so is Abraham a praying man."

"Yes, but the Lord will think Abraham is joking."

President Lincoln also turned to humor to help alleviate the strain of his office, not to mention the impact that the loss of life during the Civil War had on him. Laughter gave him a momentary break from his troubles. "I tell you the truth," he once related to a friend, "when I say that a funny story, if it has the element of genuine wit, has the same effect on me that I suppose a good square drink of whiskey has on an old toper; it puts new life into me. The fact is I have always believed that a good laugh was good for both the mental and the physical digestion." Another time he said simply: "I laugh because I must not weep—that's all, that's all."

After Lincoln became president, he mostly used his skill in telling stories for a purpose rather than for amusement. As one of his former apprentices related it, he communicated stories now largely "for business, to give a hint or enforce an argument." Here again is a skill possessed by Lincoln that was used to his utmost advantage as a leader. He realized the persuasive effects that stories had on people and once said as much during a conversation: "They say I tell a great many stories. I reckon I do; but I have learned from long experience that *plain* people, take them as they run, are more easily *influenced* through the medium of a *broad* and humorous illustration than in any other way. . . ."

Recent work in the field of leadership confirms Lincoln's strategy and emphasizes the role of stories as powerful motivational tools that spread loyalty, commitment, and enthusiasm. "All leadership is show business," wrote Peters and Austin. "It turns out that human beings reason largely by means of stories, not by mounds of data. Stories are memorable. . . . They teach. . . . If we are serious about ideals, values, motivation, commitment, we will pay attention to the role of stories [and] myths. . . ."

It's clear that Lincoln thought quite a lot about his craft of storytelling. So much so that he actually seemed to have a strategy in employing stories effectively. As the president once said:

> I believe I have the popular reputation of being a story-teller, but I do not deserve the name in its general sense, for it is not the story itself, but its purpose, or effect, that interests me. I often avoid a long and useless discussion by others or a laborious explanation on my own part by a short story that illustrates my point of view. So, too, the sharpness of a refusal or the edge of a rebuke may be blunted by an appropriate story, so as to save wounded feeling and yet serve the purpose. No, I am not simply a story-teller, but story-telling as an emollient saves me much friction and distress.

Even in the most serious moments with his cabinet members, Lincoln would take the time to tell an anecdote to illustrate to his subordinates exactly how he felt. Often, if they were discussing policy or a certain direction the country should take, the president's story would end the conversation. Other times he merely related the tale for amusement. One case in point occurred when Lincoln first showed his cabinet the original draft of the Emancipation Proclamation. After he had finished reading, Secretary Chase was bold enough to break the silence with a few suggested changes, and eventually all the members had their shot at his document. Lincoln said:

> Gentlemen, this reminds me of the story of the man who had been away from home, and when he was coming back was met by one of his farm hands, who greeted him after this fashion: "Master, the little pigs are dead, and the old sow's dead, too, but I didn't like to tell you all at once."

As a communicator, Abraham Lincoln liberally utilized stories and anecdotes, colloquial expressions, and symbols and imagery in order to influence and persuade his audience. His "down home" figures of speech attracted people, kept their attention, and, in many cases, endeared people to him. Stories were an important part of his image as a common man, and he used them so frequently that they must have been genuine. Lincoln could compare Horace Greeley to "an old shoe,—good for nothing . . . and so rotten that nothing can be done with him," or Salmon P. Chase to a "bluebottle fly, laying his eggs in every rotten spot he can find," and then turn around and tell others that "I don't amount to pig tracks in the War Department."

Yet Lincoln could also apply perfect rhyme, cadence, and alliteration to his speeches and writings. He could conceive and employ such beautiful symbolism as "the fiery trail through which we pass," "the mystic chords of memory," and "a house divided against itself cannot stand." One of the great paradoxes about Abraham Lincoln is that he could tell an off-color joke to a group of farm hands and have them in hysterical laughter, *and* he could create and deliver the Gettysburg Address, one of the most magnificent works of American literature.

Every leader must realize that the power to motivate followers resides almost solely in the ability to communicate effectively. In most business organizations, private conversation is much more important than public speaking. It provides direct contact with the individuals who are actually performing the work. Chatting informally with one or two employees will allow the leader to pick up more subtle nuances of how people actually feel and think. And *loyalty* is more often won through such personal contact than in any other way.

A contemporary leader who is introverted or shy (as Lincoln was in his youth) must make every effort to overcome this trait. A person with a great deal of talent must be capable of expressing it. He has to be able to think on his feet. And, if he cares about his employees, he can't be reticent in telling them so. He must remember that his followers want, and sometimes crave, the opportunity to simply talk to their leader. That's one reason why Franklin Roosevelt's "fireside chats" were so successful. The mere mention of the word "chat" from Roosevelt was inviting. Millions of people listened to their radio when he spoke to them and many of them probably wished he could hear them talk back.

LINCOLN PRINCIPLES

- ★ When you meet with an individual, try not to part with any unpleasant impression on either side.
- ★ Speak in simple and familiar strains with people, without any pretension of superiority. Leave people with the feeling that they've known you all their lives.
- ★ Don't forget that humor is a major component of your ability to persuade people.
- ★ A good laugh is good for both the mental and physical digestion.
- ★ Remember that people are more easily influenced through the medium of a broad and humorous illustration than in any other way.
- ★ You will often avoid a long and useless discussion by others or a laborious explanation on your own part by a short story that illustrates your point of view.
- ★ The sharpness of a refusal or the edge of a rebuke may be blunted by an appropriate story, so as to save wounded feelings and yet serve the purpose.
- ★ Loyalty is more often won through private conversation than in any other way.

All honor to Jefferson—who, in the concrete pressure of a struggle for national independence, had the coolness, forecast, and capacity to introduce . . . an abstract truth, applicable to all men and all times.

> Part of Lincoln's praise for Thomas Jefferson, one of his early heroes, to a Boston group that requested he speak there on Jefferson's birthday (April 6, 1859)

15 / *Preach a Vision and Continually Reaffirm It*

The first dictionary definition of a "leader" describes a primary shoot of a plant, the main artery through which the organism lives and thrives. In much the same way, organizations prosper or die as a result of their leader's ability to embody and communicate the company's vision. How a manager or professional influences others very much dictates the health of the department, region, and ultimately the entire organization.

All this translates into one of the major factors that distinguishes leaders from mere managers: *vision*. Peters and Austin advocated "preaching the vision": "Attention, symbols, drama," they wrote, are "the nuts and bolts of leadership. . . . You have to know where you're going. To be able to state it clearly and concisely. And you have to care about it passionately. That all adds up to vision. The concise statement or picture of where the company and its people are heading and why they should be proud of it."

Effective visions, according to Tom Peters, are inspiring. They are "clear and challenging—and about excellence." They make sense and can stand the test of time; they are stable, yet flexible. An effective vision empowers people and prepares for the future while also having roots in the past.

It's well known and documented that during the Civil War Abraham Lincoln, through his speeches, writings, and conversations, "preached a vision" of America that has never been equalled in the course of American history. Lincoln provided exactly what the country needed at that precise moment in time: a clear, concise statement of the direction of the nation and justification for the Union's drastic action in forcing civil war. In short, Lincoln provided grass-roots leadership. Everywhere he went, at every conceivable opportunity, he reaffirmed, reasserted, and reminded everyone of the basic principles upon which the nation was founded. His vision was simple, and he preached it often. It was patriotic, reverent, filled with integrity, values, and high ideals. And most importantly, it struck a chord with the American people. It was the strongest part of his bond with the *common* people.

The one most important sentiment, he felt, was "that sentiment . . . giving liberty not alone to the people of this country, but hope to the world for all future time. It was that which gave promise that in due time the weights would be lifted from the shoulders of all men, and that *all* should have an equal chance." In his July 4, 1861, message to Congress in special session, Lincoln reaffirmed his most deeply held beliefs, all of which had sprung from sentiments embodied in the Declaration of Independence:

> This is essentially a people's contest. On the side of the Union, it is a struggle for maintaining in the world that form and substance of government whose leading object is to elevate the condition of men—to lift artificial weights from all shoulders—to clear the paths

of laudable pursuit for all—to afford all an unfettered start, and a fair chance, in the race of life."

While it's true that Lincoln strategically and purposefully asserted his vision, it's also important to realize that doing so fit naturally into his overall leadership philosophy. Effective visions and organizational mission statements can't be *forced* upon the masses. Rather, they must be set in motion by means of *persuasion*. The people must accept and implement them wholeheartedly and without reservation. When this is achieved, it is always done with enthusiasm, commitment, and pride. Moreover, truly accepted visions tend to foster innovation, risk-taking, empowerment, and delegation. If the working troops understand what is expected of them, what the organization is trying to accomplish, then it becomes possible to make important decisions on lower levels, thereby creating a climate in which results and progress continually occur.

Lincoln harnessed his vision through the implementation of his own exceptional roving leadership style. He saw to it personally that the word got out. This in itself was a major accomplishment in an age when the mass communication mediums of radio and television did not yet exist. In the election year 1864, for example, the president ventured into the field to visit his battle-weary soldiers in an attempt to reinspire them; to let them know that neither he nor the nation had forgotten them; and to remind them of the importance of what they were fighting for. He told the 166th Ohio Regiment:

It is not merely for today, but for all time to come that we should perpetuate for our children's children this great and free government, which we have enjoyed all our lives. I beg you to remember this, not merely for my sake, but for yours. I happen temporarily to occupy this big White House. I am a living witness that any one of your children may look to come here as my father's child has. It is in order that each of you may have through this free government which we have enjoyed, an open field and a fair chance for your industry, enterprise, and intelligence; that you may all have equal privileges in the race of life, with all its desirable human aspirations. It is for this the struggle should be maintained. . . . The nation is worth fighting for. . . .

Lincoln preached his vision throughout the four years of his administration. His message was simple and clear, emphasizing equality and freedom (including for slaves), a "fair chance for all," and elevation of the "condition of men." This was the people's birthright, he maintained, and it should be protected and preserved for future generations.

Such inspirational words from the nation's chief executive could not help but move people, especially the common man who was the foot soldier during the Civil War. They revered Lincoln, trusted him, cheered him loudly wherever he went. The typical Union soldier enjoyed a bond with the president that few people in American history would ever have with a sitting United States president. That bond began in Washington in early 1861, when Lincoln got out of the "ivory tower" of the White House and personally visited many of the arriving troops destined for the front.

Part of this connection can also be attributed to Lincoln's "common man" image. He, too, had humble beginnings. He was raised in poverty and, in a way, he symbolized for many people the realization of the American dream. Lincoln had pulled himself up the ladder to reach the pinnacle of success. It's obvious from his speeches that Lincoln recognized this binding link he enjoyed with the common people and played on it when necessary. In fact, he made a point of tailoring his speeches so that they were easily understood. Lincoln once counseled his law partner, William Herndon, on this very matter:

Billy, don't shoot too high—aim lower and the common people will understand you. They are the ones you
want to reach—at least they are the ones you ought to
reach. The educated and refined people will understand
you any way. If you aim too high your ideas will go
over the heads of the masses and only hit those who
need no hitting.

Through the course of the four years of the Civil War,
Lincoln kept repeating and renewing his vision so that it
would not diminish in meaning. It was this process of renewal
that was, in effect, Lincoln's greatest form of motivation. Over
time, as values decay and incentives dwindle, leaders must
constantly provide a rejuvenating process. In Lincoln's case, the
fight against slavery was already an age-old issue, and the Civil
War was a culmination of decades of conflict. It was time to
renew and regenerate old values. Lincoln strategically applied
himself to this task. He resurrected the Declaration of Independence, dusted off the Constitution, and brought back a sense of
pride and patriotism that had not been seen since the days of the
American Revolution. Lincoln revitalized the old values of
Americanism and reminded all citizens why the United States
was formed in the first place, just as all leaders should remind
subordinates why *their* organization was formed in the first place.

When effecting renewal, Lincoln called on the *past*, related
it to the *present*, and then used them both to provide a link to
the *future*. A perfect example of Lincoln's interweaving the
concepts of vision and renewal is illustrated in his immortal
Gettysburg Address. Long regarded as one of the great works
of American literature and critically acclaimed for its simplicity
and directness, the speech was delivered at the dedication of
the Gettysburg National Cemetery only four months after
one of the most important Union victories of the Civil War.
While Lincoln technically spent only a few weeks preparing
the address, it's clear from his past oratory and writings that all
of the concepts, and many of the phrases employed, had been

part of his vision for the nation for years. This time, however, Lincoln was unusually eloquent, perhaps because of the significance of the battle itself or perhaps because of the reverence of the occasion.

Whatever the reason, Lincoln was unusually committed to attending the ceremony and making his speech. He left Washington amid the anguished protests of his wife, Mary, because their youngest son was ill and confined to bed. She felt his place was at their boy's side. And for Lincoln, who had already watched two sons die from disease, this was not an unimportant matter. But the president decided to make the trip anyway, hoping that the sturdy ten-year-old Tad would recover. There would be no holding back Lincoln, who was committed to delivering his important message to the American public, and this would be a perfect opportunity to do so.

On November 19, 1863, after having had his mind greatly eased by receipt of a telegram relating that his son was much improved, and after listening to the principal orator of the day, Edward Everett, speak for nearly two hours, Abraham Lincoln spent only two minutes reminding the nation what the Civil War, and America itself, was all about:

[The Past]
Four score and seven years ago our fathers brought forth on this continent, a new nation, conceived in Liberty, and dedicated to the proposition that all men are created equal.

[The Present]
Now we are engaged in a great civil war; testing whether that nation, or any nation so conceived and so dedicated, can long endure. We are met on a great battle-field of that war. We have come to dedicate a portion of that field, as a final resting place for those who gave their lives that that nation might live. It is altogether fitting and proper that we should do this.

[Renewal]

But, in a larger sense, we can not dedicate—we can not consecrate—we can not hallow—this ground. The brave men, living and dead, who struggled here have consecrated it, far above our poor power to add or detract. The world will little note, nor long remember what we say here, but it can never forget what they did here. It is for us the living, rather, to be dedicated here to the unfinished work which they who fought here have thus far so nobly advanced. It is rather for us to be here dedicated to the great task remaining before us—that from these honored dead we take increased devotion to that cause for which they gave the last full measure of devotion—that we here highly resolve that these dead shall not have died in vain—that this nation, under God, shall have a new birth of freedom—

[The Future]

and that government of the people, by the people, for the people, shall not perish from the earth.

Renewal of America's vision by Lincoln provided a kind of physical reinforcement, more powerful than sending troops to the field, or guns and supplies to the soldiers. It tended to put everyone on a dynamic and forceful upward spiral of action and commitment. It was far more powerful than throwing money and people at the problem. By clearly renewing his vision and then gaining acceptance and commitment, Lincoln essentially revved up, and then released, what amounted to a battalion of energy within each person. Without question, Lincoln realized what every leader must—that the process of renewal releases the critical human talent and energy that is necessary to insure success.

LINCOLN PRINCIPLES

★ Provide a clear, concise statement of the direction of your organization, and justify the actions you take.

★ Everywhere you go, at every conceivable opportunity, reaffirm, reassert, and remind everyone of the basic principles upon which your organization was founded.

★ Effective visions can't be forced on the masses. Rather, you must set them in motion by means of persuasion.

★ Harness your vision through implementation of your own personal roving leadership style.

★ When you preach your vision, don't shoot too high. Aim lower and the common people will understand you. They are the ones you want to reach—at least they are the ones you ought to reach.

★ When effecting renewal, call on the *past*, relate it to the *present*, and then use them both to provide a link to the *future*.

★ You must realize that the process of renewal releases the critical human talent and energy necessary to insure success.

Epilogue

Although the true genius of Abraham Lincoln's leadership ability has often been overlooked, during his lifetime there were a few key people, mostly in his inner circle, who did grasp and appreciate the depth of his skills. Secretary of State William H. Seward acknowledged his "executive force and vigor," while War Secretary Edwin M. Stanton realized that he would "belong to the ages." Even newspaperman Horace Greeley, often at odds with the president and his administration, came to value Lincoln's excellence:

> He was not a born king of men . . . but a child of the common people, who made himself a great persuader, therefore a leader, by dint of firm resolve, patient effort, and dogged perseverance. He slowly won his way to eminence and fame by doing the work that lay next to him—doing it with all his growing might—doing it as

well as he could, and learning by his failure, when failure was encountered, how to do it better. . . . He was open to all impressions and influences, and gladly profited by the teachings of events and circumstances, no matter how adverse or unwelcome. There was probably no year of his life when he was not a wiser, cooler, and better man than he had been the year preceding.

Greeley and some of Lincoln's other contemporaries clearly understood his real ability. Unfortunately, after Lincoln's assassination came martyrdom and creation of the "Lincoln Myth." As a result, Lincoln's true leadership talent—his style, substance, and philosophy—has been lost, obscured, even overlooked through the years.

Lincoln was extraordinarily self-confident and possessed great persuasive and political skills that were developed over his lifetime. When civil war broke out, as president of the United States he took charge and enhanced the government's executive function and responsibility. He did not intend to significantly change the office of the presidency, which, of course, is exactly what he did. Rather, the transformation came about as a consequence of his leadership during the war, his aggressiveness in taking "the bull by the horns" and in utilizing any means necessary to preserve the nation, such as exploiting the emergency powers granted him under the Constitution of the United States. As Greeley said, Lincoln learned and profited from experience while on the job. He cultivated passion and trust in all of his followers—delegating rather than trying to do it all himself, coaching rather than dictating. Yet, at the same time, he immersed himself in the details of the war effort. He learned how to become a commander-in-chief. He mastered military tactics and strategy. As a Washington outsider, he quickly grasped an understanding of the general organization of the United States

Government and how to work within it. In short, Lincoln, by his own design, actually *grew* into the job of the presidency.

In order to comprehend modern leadership theory and be successful in the future, leaders must look to the past—to President Abraham Lincoln, for example—who *routinely* practiced nearly all of the "revolutionary thinking" techniques that have been preached to American industry in the last ten to fifteen years. Lincoln can be looked to as the ideal model for desirable, effective leadership. He is a perfect example of what James MacGregor Burns termed a "transforming leader"—a person who aims for the evolution of a new level of awareness and understanding among all members of an organization. Such a leader rejects the use of naked power and instead attempts to motivate and mobilize followers by persuading them to take ownership of their roles in a more grand mission that is shared by all members of the organization.

Lincoln's grand mission, his "common purpose," was essentially the American experiment and the ideals expressed in the Declaration of Independence. He aimed at the "elevation of men," opposed anything that tended to degrade them, and especially lashed out at the institution of slavery. And it was slavery that was at the heart of the South's attempted separation from the Union. He played upon the degradation of slavery and its lack of human dignity. By vehemently opposing it, and appealing to the "better angels of our nature," Lincoln was able to mobilize his followers in a common mission. He also knew the dire consequences of allowing the South to secede from the United States. In May 1861, he remarked to John Hay: "We must settle this question now, whether in a free government, the minority have the right to break up the government whenever they choose. If we fail, it will go far to prove the incapability of the people to govern themselves."

It was Abraham Lincoln who, during the most difficult period in the nation's history, almost single-handedly preserved the American concept of government. Had he not been the leader that he was, secession in 1860 could have led to further partitioning of the country into an infinite number of smaller, separate pieces, some retaining slavery, some not. He accomplished this task with a naturalness and intuitiveness in leading people that was at least a century ahead of his time.

Lincoln knew that true leadership is often realized by exerting quiet and subtle influence on a day-to-day basis, by frequently seeing followers and other people face to face. He treated everyone with the same courtesy and respect, whether they were kings or commoners. He lifted people out of their everyday selves and into a higher level of performance, achievement, and awareness. He obtained extraordinary results from ordinary people by instilling purpose in their endeavors. He was open, civil, tolerant, and fair, and he maintained a respect for the dignity of all people at all times. Lincoln's attitude and behavior as president of the United States essentially characterized the process that symbolizes acceptable and decent relations among human beings. Abraham Lincoln was the essence of leadership.

Notes

Preface

Burns, p. 427.

Introduction

Burns, p. 19, p. 50, p. 58; Freud quote from Strozier, p. 3 (Strozier also notes
Lincoln's attachment to his stepmother and estrangement from his father); "a
model child" from Neely, p. 187; "keeping forty acres of land" from CW, vol.
II, p. 111, and Neely, p. 187; Lincoln's visit to his mother from Lamon (1872),
pp. 462–463; task "greater than that which rested on Washington" from CW,
vol. IV, p. 190; "bunglingly sign his own name" from CW, vol. IV, p. 61; "more
painful than pleasant" from CW, vol. II, p. 97; Burns's observations of other
leaders, pp. 54–112; activity in the Congress prior to inauguration, from
Congressional Globe, 36th Congress., 2nd sess., pp. 46, 1001, 1225–32, and
Fehrenbacher; "if slavery is not wrong" from CW, vol. VII, p. 281; Civil War
"in their hands" from CW, vol. IV, p. 271; First Inaugural quote from CW, vol.
IV, p. 264.

Lesson #1

Opening epigraph from CW, vol. IV, p. 513; Peters and Waterman, p. 122; Peters and Austin, pp. 31–32; "75 percent of his time meeting people" from Oates, p. 266; "welcome visitor anyway" from Oates, p. 265; "come among them without fear" from Oates, p. 453; "burst in on one of his cabinet members" from *Lincoln Day by Day* (DD), vol. III, p. 86; spending nights in Telegraph Office from Bates, p. 160; "on Stanton's sofa" from Williams, p. 123; "rumors about General Grant" from Williams, p. 316; "see you if you call" from CW, vol. VII, p. 10; "public opinion baths" from Sandburg, *The War Years*, vol. I, p. 237; "all [who] claim the personal acquaintance" from Villard, pp. 39–40; "everyone likes a compliment" from CW, vol. VII, p. 356; "stand a good deal when they are flattered" from Hertz, p. 597; "if they can stand it" from Oates, p. 418; "gives good honest hearty shake" from DD, vol. III, p. 48; "riding horse along the lines of troops" from DD, vol. III, pp. 114, 126; "given greatest credit" from CW, vol. VIII, p. 75; "visiting wounded" from DD, vol. III, pp. 57–58; Lt. Worden visit from DD, vol. III, p. 186; "funeral for eighteen women" from DD, vol. III, pp. 121, 266; "attending a working session of Senate" from DD, vol. III, p. 82; "sending Blair and Meigs to Missouri" from Neely, p. 119; "Henry Stoddard" from DD, vol. III, p. 137; "Haupt" from DD, vol. III, p. 194; "H. E. Wing" from DD, vol. III, p. 257; "troops break into cheers" from Oates, pp. 457–458; "visit to Seward" from Oates, p. 459.

Lesson #2

Opening epigraph from CW, vol. II, pp. 461, 468; Bennis and Nanus, pp. 32, 46, 67; Peters and Austin, pp. 266, 333; Iacocca, p. 54; "I must do it" from CW, vol. IV, pp. 316–318; "one war at a time" from Thomas, p. 299; "President best of us" from Thomas, p. 269; "no token of any intelligent understanding" from Neely, p. 287; "Stanton greets Lincoln" from Oates, pp. 458–459; "Robert's recollection of Stanton" from Neely, p. 289; "I can do it all" from Dennett, p. 33; "isn't he a rare bird" from Williams, p. 45; "making points of etiquette and personal dignity" from Dennett, pp. 34–35; "McClellan's letter to Lincoln" from Williams, p. 65; Burnside quote from Williams, p. 110; "actual war coming" from CW, vol. VI, p. 500; bulldog story from Hertz, p. 357; "Human action can be modified" from CW, vol. III, p. 541; "extinguish hope" from CW, vol. V, p. 330; "people not suspected of disloyalty" from CW, vol. VII, p. 284.

Lesson #3

Opening epigraph from CW, vol. III, p. 27; Definition of Leadership from Burns, p. 417; "discourage litigation" from CW, vol. II, p. 81; "when the conduct of men" from CW, vol. I, p. 273; "no man is good enough" from CW, vol. II, p. 266; "familiarize yourselves with the chains of bondage" from CW, vol. III, p. 95; "understanding the spirit of our institutions" from CW, vol. III, p. 380; "consultation with the head of that department" from CW, vol. VII, p. 423; "we must not fight till you are ready" from Dennett, p. 31; "I will hold McClellan's horse" from Thomas, p. 307; "Grant is the first general I have had" from Oates, p. 418; McClellan (10-13-63) from CW, vol. V, p. 461; Halleck (9-19-63) from CW, vol. VI, p. 467; Burnside (9-27-63) from CW, vol. VI, p. 484; Banks (1-13-64) from CW, vol. VII, p. 124; Grant (4-30-64) from CW, vol. VII, p. 324; story about the Italian captain from Hertz, pp. 221–222; "Hooker suggesting country needed a dictator" from Neely, p. 151; Hooker letter from CW, vol. VI, pp. 78–79; "just such a letter a father might write to his son" from Neely, p. 151.

Lesson #4

Opening epigraph from CW, vol. VI, p. 230; "store winked out" from CW, vol. IV, p. 65; "the national debt" from Neely, p. 23; "Myths which displace truth" from Seldes, p. 324; Peters, *Thriving on Chaos*, p. 519; Bennis and Nanus, p. 21; Burns, p. 389; "pursuit of liberty" and "equality" from Burns, p. 449; "never had a feeling politically" from CW, vol. IV, p. 240; "one hard nut to crack" from CW, vol. II, pp. 240–241; "people's contest" from CW, vol. IV, p. 438; "stand with anybody that stands right" from CW, vol. II, p. 273; "never add the weight of your character" from CW, vol. I, pp. 383–384; "it decorates the ruin it makes" from Hertz, p. 586; "criminal and revolver" story from Hertz, p. 338, Zall, p. 154; "majestic-looking tree" story from Hertz, pp. 362–364, Zall, pp. 155–156; "it is your duty to advance the aims of your organization" from CW, vol. IV, p. 202; "can't fool all of the people" from McClure, p. 124.

Lesson #5

Opening epigraph from CW, vol. V, p. 346; "adopt new views so fast" from CW, vol. V, pp. 388–389; "cowardly pair of legs" from Boller, p. 139;

"unwilling for any boy under 18 to be shot" from CW, vol. VI, p. 506; "doll Jack" from Thomas, p. 319; "when neither incompetency nor intentional wrong" from Neely, p. 60; "planting and cultivating thorns" from CW, vol. VII, p. 255; meeting at Hampton Roads conversation from Lamon, p. 127; "frighten them out of the country" from Thomas, p. 544; Sherman quote from Neely, p. 60; "unbeknownst-like" story from Hertz, pp. 369–370; "asking for Dixie" from CW, vol. VIII, p. 393; "with malice toward none" from CW, vol. VIII, p. 333; "ruined for slight causes" from CW vol. VI, p. 335; "better angels of our nature" from CW, vol. VII, p. 255.

Lesson #6

Opening epigraph from CW, vol. III, p. 550; "craftiest and most dishonest politician" from Boller, *Campaigns*, p. 102; "I have reached this city" from CW, vol. IV, p. 247; "I must make nineteen enemies" from Hertz, pp. 256–257; "in any future great national trial" from CW, vol. VIII, p. 101; "young man who has been the subject of envy and malice" from Hertz, pp. 637–638; "sit on the blister" from Hertz, pp. 295–296; "abstain from reading reports" from CW, vol. VIII, p. 401; "I am not going to be terrified" from Lamon, p. 23; "not entirely safe" from CW, vol. III, p. 401; "the shepherd drives the wolf" from CW, vol. VII, p. 302; Antietam episode from Lamon, pp. 141–144; "more apt to amuse him " from CW, vol. III, p. 13; "steamboat whistle" story from Hertz, p. 44, Zall, p. 118; "boy and ship" story from Lamon, pp. 139–140, Zall. p. 111; "the pioneers in any movement" from Hertz, p. 343; "no human being" from CW, vol. II, p. 89; "it often requires more courage" from Hertz, pp. 139–140; "he who has the right" from CW, vol. VI, p. 383; "truth is generally the best vindication against slander" from CW, vol. VII, p. 440; "do the very best you know how" from Sandburg, *War Years*, vol. II, p. 237; "yield to even one false charge" from CW, vol. VI, p. 230; "beware of being assailed" from CW, vol. VI, p. 234; "the probability that you may fail" from CW, vol. I, p. 178.

Lesson #7

Opening epigraphs from CW, vol. IV, p. 261; vol. V, p. 92; vol. V, p. 304; vol. V, p. 166; Burns, pp. 243–244; "if it can consistently be done" from CW, vol. IV, p. 517; "you think it is not inconsistent" from CW, vol. V, p. 177; "not best to swap horses" from CW, vol. VII, p. 384; "my policy is to have no policy" from Sandburg, *War Years*, vol. I, p. 211; "I shall not surrender this game" from CW, vol. V, p. 343; "an opportunity for a change of mind" from Dennett, p. 11; "I shall do less" from CW, vol. V, pp. 388–389; Peters, pp. 391–397; "I was in such deep distress" from CW, vol. VI, p. 327; "never sent, or signed" from CW, vol. VI, p. 328; "damn Jonesboro" from Bates, p. 202; "not sent" from CW, vol. VI, pp. 480–481; "let minor differences go to the winds" from CW, vol. II, p. 390; "what they want is a squabble and a fuss" from CW, vol. IV, p. 38; "I never remember the past against him" from Dennett, p. 234; "quarrel not at all" from CW, vol. VI, p. 538.

Lesson #8

Opening epigraph from CW, vol. VII, p. 189; "my oath imposed upon me" from CW, vol. VII, pp. 281–282; Aesop parable from Hertz, p. 262, Zall, pp. 77–78; Fehrenbacher, p. 8; "order to Chase to spend $2 million" from CW, vol. V, p. 242; "purchase of twenty steamships" from CW, vol. V, pp. 240–243; "appropriate money for *habeas corpus*" from CW, vol. IV, pp. 368–369; "money to encourage immigration" from CW, vol. VII, p. 489; "make short reports" from CW, vol. VI, p. 320; tightrope story from Hertz, p. 263; "Preliminary Emancipation Proclamation" quote from CW, vol. V, p. 434; "response to Chase about Proclamation" from Thomas, p. 381; "statement about Wade-Davis Bill" from CW, vol. VII, p. 433; "Presidential chin-fly" story from Hertz, p. 226, Zall, p. 29; "memo to Chase" from CW, vol. VII, p. 419; Lincoln's response to senators from Oates, p. 424; "give him a chance" from Thomas, p. 519; "buckhorn chair" from Welles, vol. II, p. 196; Lincoln's note to Blair from CW, vol. VIII, p. 18; John F. Kennedy quote from *Profiles In Courage*, p. 20; "ballots and bullets" from CW, vol. IV, p. 439.

Lesson #9

Opening epigraph from CW, vol. VIII, pp. 181–182; "I claim not to have controlled events" from CW, vol. VII, p. 282; Lao Tzu quoted in Bennis and Nanus, p. 152; "Chase episode" from Thomas, pp. 371–374, Oates, pp. 356–358; "the order was mine" from Lamon, p. 202; "the honor will be his quote" from CW, vol. VI, p. 518; letter to Grant from CW, vol. VI, p. 326; letter to Sherman from CW, vol. VIII, pp. 181–182; Sherman's response from CW, vol. VIII, p. 182; "No part of the honor" from CW, vol. VIII, p. 400; "if your commanders can't be successful" from CW, vol. V, p. 359;

"organization does not depend on the life of any one individual" from Hertz, p. 229; "greatest credit" from CW, vol. VIII, p. 75.

Lesson #10

Opening epigraph from CW, vol. VI, p. 257; "little engine that knew no rest" from Herndon and Weik, p. 304; "thirsts and burns for distinction" from CW, vol. I, p. 114; "the cause of civil liberty" from CW, vol. III, p. 339; "I am neither dead nor dying" from CW, vol. III, p. 346; "visiting the War Department" from Thomas, p. 498; "delay is ruining us" from CW, vol. V, p. 92; "time is everything" from CW, vol. V, p. 304; "purpose to be just and fair" from CW, vol. VI, p. 391; "He who does something" from CW, vol. V, p. 85; "ploughing the stumps" story from Zall, p. 74; recent studies in leadership from Bennis and Nanus, pp. 28, 45; "my dog is always mad" story from Zall, p. 76; "leave nothing for tomorrow" from CW, vol. II, p. 81; "your war will not be won by strategy alone" from CW, vol. V, p. 484; "watch it every day" from CW, vol. VII, p. 476; "half-finished work" from CW, vol. I, p.5.

Lesson #11

Opening epigraph from Oates, pp. 325–326; "you are green" from Reports of the Committee on the Conduct of the War, 1863, vol. II, p. 36; "General War Order #1" from CW, vol. V, p. 111; Hay's comments from Dennett, p. 36; "Lincoln made decision himself" from Dennett, pp. 37–38, "letter to McClellan" from CW, vol. V, p. 185; Chase's comment from Williams, pp. 91–92, Oates, p. 326; "thinking of taking the field" from Thomas, p. 309; "authorizing Halleck to remove McClellan" from Pease and Randall, p. 563; "victory complete" from Williams, p. 169; "Lincoln's visit to McClellan" from Williams, p. 172; "McClellan's bodyguard" from Sandburg, *War Years*, vol. I, p. 595; "sore-tongued and fatigued horses" from CW, vol. V, p. 474; "the slows" from Sandburg, vol. I, p. 491; "first-rate clerk" from Dennett, p. 176; "McClernand's smear campaign against Grant" from Williams, p. 190, 218; "I can't spare this man" from Williams, p. 86; "reprimand to Banks" from CW, vol. V, pp. 505–506; "confused and stunned like a duck hit on the head" from Dennett, p. 106; "Lincoln's visit to Burnside" from Williams, p. 194, 197, 200; "stuck in the mud" from Oates, p. 367; "Hooker is overconfident" from Oates, p. 375; "Lincoln's letters to Hooker" from CW, vol. VI, pp. 201, 217; "Lincoln's refusal" from Williams, p. 246; "a want of alacrity to obey" from Welles, vol. I, p. 348; "fight well on his own dunghill" from Williams, p. 260; "is that all" from Williams, p. 265; "the whole country is our soil" from Dennett, p. 67; "Lincoln's comments to Welles," from Welles, vol. I, p. 370; "the service he did at Gettysburg" from Dennett, p. 69; "I could have whipped them myself" from Dennett, p. 67; "old woman trying to shoo her geese across a creek" from Sandburg, vol. II, p. 436; "Lincoln counseling Grant" from Williams, p. 299; "the monkey and his tail" story from Zall, p. 86; "those not skinning can hold a leg" from Dennett, p. 179; "drawn up the ladder" from Sandburg, vol. III, p. 43; Grant quote from Oates, p. 420; "the dogged pertinacity of Grant that wins" from Dennett, p. 180; "chew and choke" from CW, vol. VII, p. 499; Grant comment from Williams, p. 335; "as if he had inherited it" from Williams, p. 321; "journey had done him good" from Welles, vol. II, p. 58; "Lincoln's meeting at Fortress Monroe with Grant" from Oates, p. 428; "follow the confederates to the death" from Williams, p. 331; "had to sustain the sinking courage" from Dennett, p. 176; "let the *thing* be pressed" from CW, vol. VIII, p. 392.

Lesson #12

Opening epigraph from CW, vol. V, p. 537; "if we never try" from CW, vol. V, p. 461; "I have not lost a particle of confidence" from Williams, p. 23; Peters, pp. 191–279; "swearing for the regiment" story from Hertz, pp. 531–532; "Lincoln's patent" from Neely, p. 162; "patent system" from CW, vol. III, p. 363; "Hyde rocket explosion" from DD, vol. III, p. 150; "breech-loading rifle demonstration at cabinet meeting" from Bruce, pp. 252–257; "order of 25,000 breechloaders" from DD, vol. III, p. 71; "order for 10,000 Spensers" from DD, vol. III, p. 85.

Lesson #13

Opening epigraph from CW, vol. II, p. 81; Douglas quote from Forney, vol. II, p. 179; "175 speeches, many of them extemporaneous" from Braden, p. 55; "Lincoln would bend his knees" from Oates, p. 166; "never considered anything finished" from Braden, p. 55; Nicolay and Hay comments from Nicolay and Hay, vol. II, p. 136; "Republican Principles" from Oates, p. 158; "reporter's comments on Cooper Institute speech" from McClure, pp. 306–307; "Cooper Institute speech" quotes from CW, vol. III, pp. 547, 550; "Lincoln's comment" from Fairchild, p. 139; "Farewell Address" from

CW, vol. IV, p. 190; "I am neither to write or speak" from CW, vol. IV, p. 80; "kindly let me be silent" from CW, vol. IV, p. 91; "in my present position" from CW, vol. V, p. 450; "try not to make mistakes" from CW, vol. VIII, p. 394; "your troubles are over" from Oates, p. 211; Herndon quote from Basler, p. 47; Burns, p. 44; Iacocca, p. 53; Peters and Austin, p. 330; Bennis and Nanus, pp. 39, 43.

Lesson #14

Opening epigraph from Hertz, p. 630; Thurlow Weed comment from Thomas, p. 485; "Lincoln to Weed" from CW, vol. VI, p. 514; Schurz quote from Schurz, p. 253; "Abraham is joking" story from Sandburg, vol. III, p. 367; "a good laugh" from Sandburg, vol. III, p. 305; "must not weep" from Whitney, p. 131; "quote from Lincoln's former apprentice" from Zall, p. 5; Peters and Austin, pp. 278, 281; "I believe I have the popular reputation of being a story-teller" from Hertz, pp. 638–639; "little pigs are dead" story from Zall, p. 157; "an old shoe" from Welles, vol. II, p. 112; "bluebottle fly" from Dennett, p. 110; "I don't amount to pig tracks" from Sandburg, vol. II, p. 305.

Lesson #15

Opening epigraph from CW, vol. III, p. 376; Peters and Austin, p. 284; Peters, *Thriving on Chaos*, pp. 399–404; "all should have an equal chance" from CW, vol. IV, pp. 240–242; "people's contest" from CW, vol. IV, p. 438; "comments to 166th Ohio Regiment" from CW, vol. VII, p. 512; "Billy, don't shoot too high" comment from Herndon, p. 262; "Gettysburg Address" from CW, vol. VII, p. 21; "renewal releases the critical human talent and energy" from Gardner, pp. 121–137.

Epilogue

Greeley quote from Thomas, p. 524; "transforming leader" from Burns, p. 4; "remark to John Hay" from Dennett, pp. 18–19.

Bibliography

Basler, Roy P. 1946. *Abraham Lincoln: His Speeches and Writings*. World Publishing Co., New York.

Basler, Roy P. ed. 1953. *The Collected Works of Abraham Lincoln*. 8 vols. Rutgers Univ. Press, New Brunswick, New Jersey. In the notes, coded as CW.

Bates, David H. 1939. *Lincoln in the Telegraph Office*. D. Appleton-Century Company, New York.

Bennis, Warren, and Burt Nanus. 1985. *Leaders*. Perennial Library, Harper & Row, New York.

Boller, Paul F., Jr. 1981. *Presidential Anecdotes*. Oxford Univ. Press, New York.

Boller, Paul F., Jr. 1984. *Presidential Campaigns*. Oxford Univ. Press, New York.

Boatner, Mark M., III. 1988. *Civil War Dictionary*. David McKay, New York.

Braden, Waldo W. 1988. *Abraham Lincoln: Public Speaker*. Louisiana State Univ. Press, Baton Rouge.

Bruce, Robert V. 1960. *President Lincoln and Weapons Policy*, in *Lincoln for the Ages*, ed. by Ralph G. Newman, Doubleday, New York.

Burns, James MacGregor. 1978. *Leadership*. Harper & Row, New York.

CW. See Basler, Roy P. 1953.

DD. See Miers, Earl S., ed.

Dennett, Tyler, ed. 1939. *The Diaries and Letters of John Hay*. Dodd, Mead & Company, New York.

Fairchild, Johnson E. 1960. *Lincoln at Cooper Union*, in *Lincoln for the Ages*, ed. by Ralph G. Newman, Doubleday, New York.

Fehrenbacher, Don E. 1987. *Lincoln's Wartime Leadership: The First Hundred Days*. Journal of the Abraham Lincoln Assn., Springfield, Ill. Vol. 9, pp. 1–18.

Forney, John W. 1881. *Anecdotes of Public Men*. New York.

Gardner, John W. 1990. *On Leadership*. Free Press, New York.

Herndon, William H., and Jesse W. Weik. 1930. *Herndon's Life of Lincoln*, ed. by Paul M. Angle. World Publishing Co., Cleveland.

Hertz, Emmanuel. 1939. *Lincoln Talks: A Biography in Anecdote*. Halcyon House, New York.

Iacocca, Lee. 1984. *Iacocca: An Autobiography*. Bantam Books, New York.

Kennedy, John F. 1955. *Profiles in Courage*. Harper, New York.

Lamon, Ward H. 1872. *The Life of Abraham Lincoln: From His Birth to His Inauguration as President*. James E. Osgood, Chicago.

Lamon, Ward H. 1895. *Recollections of Abraham Lincoln: 1847–1865*. A. C. McClurg, Chicago.

McClure, Alexander K. 1901. *Abe Lincoln's Yarns and Stories*. Winston, Philadelphia.

Miers, Earl S., ed. 1969. *Lincoln Day by Day*. U.S. Government Publication, Washington, D.C. In the notes, coded as DD.

Neely, Mark E., Jr. 1982. *The Abraham Lincoln Encyclopedia*. McGraw-Hill, New York.

Nicolay, John G., and Hay, John. 1904. *Abraham Lincoln: History*. 10 vols., New York.

Oates, Stephen B. 1977. *With Malice Toward None*. Harper & Row, New York.

Pease, T. C., and Randall, J. G. 1927. *Diary of Orville Hickman Browning*. Springfield.

Peters, Thomas J., and Robert H. Waterman. 1982. *In Search of Excellence*. Harper & Row, New York.

Peters, Thomas, J., and Nancy K. Austin. 1985. *A Passion for Excellence*. Random House, New York.

Peters, Thomas J. 1987. *Thriving on Chaos*. Alfred A. Knopf, New York.

Reports of the Committee on the Conduct of the War. 1863. Washington, D.C. Vol. II, p. 36.

Sandburg, Carl. 1936–1939. *Abraham Lincoln: The War Years*. Harcourt, Brace & World, New York.

Schurz, Carl. 1907. "Reminiscences of a Long Life," in *McClure's Magazine*, vol. XXVIII (January).

Seldes, George. 1960. *The Great Quotations*. Citadel Press, New Jersey.

Strozier, Charles B. 1983. *Lincoln's Quest for Union*. Basic Books, New York.

Thomas, Benjamin P. 1952. *Abraham Lincoln*. Alfred A. Knopf, New York.

Villard, Henry. 1941. *Lincoln on the Eve of '61*. Alfred A. Knopf, New York.

Welles, Gideon. 1911. *The Diary of Gideon Welles*. Houghton Mifflin, Boston.

Whitney, Henry Clay. 1940. *Life on the Circuit with Lincoln*. Caxton Printers, Caldwell, Idaho.

Williams, T. Harry. 1952. *Lincoln and His Generals*. Alfred A. Knopf, New York.

Zall, P. M. 1982. *Abe Lincoln Laughing*. Univ. of California Press, Berkeley.

INDEX